NEW BRITAIN
LIFEBOATS
AN ILLUSTRATED HISTORY OF
150 YEARS OF GALLANTRY

Nicholas Leach
FOXGLOVE PUBLISHING

Above: Hovercraft H-005 Hurley Spirit on exercise off New Brighton Promenade. (Nicholas Leach)

Cover: (upper) New Brighton's first motor lifeboat William and Kate Johnston; (lower) the present New Brighton lifeboat, Atlantic 85 Charles Dibdin (Civil Service No.51) (B-837). (Nicholas Leach)

Page 1: Atlantic 85 Charles Dibdin (Civil Service No.51) on a training exercise in the Mersey. (Nicholas Leach)

First published 2015

Foxglove Publishing Ltd
Foxglove House
Shute Hill
Lichfield WS13 8DB
United Kingdom
Tel 01543 673594

ISBN 9781909540040

Typesetting and origination by Nicholas Leach

Printed in Great Britain

Acknowledgements

Many people have assisted with this project to produce a comprehensive history of the famous and important New Brighton lifeboat station, and I am very grateful to them all. Station archivist and former Honorary Secretary and crew member Frank Brereton answered numerous queries and questions, and supplied many interesting and unusual photos; without his input the book could not have been completed, and I am extremely grateful for his time and help. Thanks also to Mike Jones, who has also been very helpful and keen to assist throughout; and to Station Press Officer Bob Warwick, who supplied some up-to-date photos. At the RNLI, Nathan Williams supplied several images, and I am grateful for his continued assistance. Barry Cox, Honorary Librarian, and the RNLI Heritage Team have facilitated my research, and I am also grateful to them. Thanks to Jeff Morris, Honorary Archivist of the Lifeboat Enthusiasts' Society, who allowed me to use information from his previous histories of the station and supplied photographs for possible inclusion; and to Martin Fish for supplying his photos. NL

Contents

	Introduction	5
1770s – 1863	Liverpool's Early Life-savers	7
	BOX Perch Rock Fort and Lighthouse 10	
1863 – 1898	The RNLI Establishes a Station	14
	BOX The lifeboat trials at Lowestoft 30	
1893 – 1923	Steam Lifeboats	35
1898 – 1936	The Sailing Lifeboats	49
1923 – 1950	William and Kate Johnston	53
	BOX Service Listing for 1940 73	
1950 – 1973	Norman B. Corlett	87
1973 –	Atlantic Lifeboats	109
	BOX Bev Brown's memories 114	
2004 –	Flying to the rescue	172
	Appendices	183

A Lifeboat summary 183
B Lifeboat details 185
C Summary of services 1863–1973 189
D Summary of inshore lifeboat services 193
E Tractors and launch vehicles 194
F Personnel summary 196

NEW BRIGHTON and the RIVER MERSEY

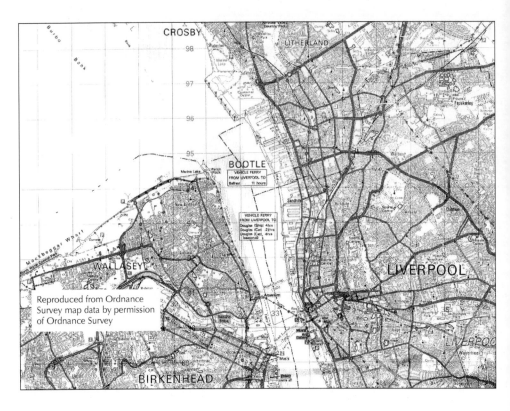

Reproduced from Ordnance
Survey map data by permission
of Ordnance Survey

Lifeboat stations around the Mersey

[Listed in geographical order]

West Kirby	1966 –
Hilbre Island*	1848 – 1939
Hoylake*	1803 –
New Brighton	1863 –
Magazines*	1827 – 1863
Liverpool*	1802 – 1894
Formby*	c1776 – 1889 and
	1892 - 1919
Southport*	1840 – 1925

*Stations established and operated by
the Liverpool Dock Trust/Mersey Docks
and Harbours Board

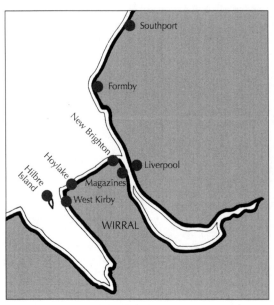

Introduction

New Brighton lifeboat station is situated at the entrance to the river Mersey, facing the Port of Liverpool, one of the country's largest, busiest and most important ports. In the national history of lifeboats and life-saving, the Mersey played a significant part, as the first organised lifeboat service in the world was developed, funded and organised by the Liverpool Dock Trustees in the 1770s to safeguard shipping at the entrance to the river and using the then expanding dock system.

Although the RNLI did not establish a lifeboat station at New Brighton until the 1860s, at a time when life-saving provision was being expanded around the country, the station is one of the most important and significant, mainly because it has not conformed to standard lifeboat operation and the crews, on whom exceptional demands were made by the busy nature of the area they served, have preferred non-standard lifeboat types. During the nineteenth century the station was one of only four which operated the unusual Tubular design of pulling and sailing lifeboat, a type deemed particularly suitable to the Mersey and its environs.

When the Tubular was replaced in the 1890s, as if to emphasize the importance of the station a steam lifeboat was built for service

Plaque mounted on a stone plinth outside the current lifeboat house recording the work of the conventional lifeboats and the ILBs to 1991. (Nicholas Leach)

An aeriel view of New Brighton from the 1950s showing the pier at the far left and, in the centre, the Tower Ballroom, which was damaged by fire in 1969 and subsequently demolished. The lifeboat is to the right of the pier on moorings. The wooded area on the riverfront (upper right) is Magazines, the area of the first lifeboat station in the area. Foreground left is the Marine Lake, with, to the right, New Brighton Bathing Pool, once the biggest open-air pool in Europe. The current station was built across road from the Pool, to the right in this photo; a Mossirons supermarket was built on the site of the Pool.

in and around the Mersey as it was recognised that the station needed a large lifeboat to cope with the demands made on it. Next, with the advent of the motor lifeboat in the early years of the twentieth century, New Brighton was at the forefront of developments when the first twin-engined and twin-screw motor lifeboat was sent to the Mersey in the 1920s. The stationing of the impressive *William and Kate Johnston* in the Mersey was proof of the importance of the New Brighton station, something that was further emphasised when a second motor lifeboat arrived in 1938 to cover the busy Mersey during its boom years.

The volunteer crews had to be adaptable and able to deal with change when the status of the station was changed in the 1970s and the offshore lifeboat was replaced by an Atlantic rigid-inflatable type. Then in its infancy in terms of development, the Atlantic type has since proved to be an exceptionally capable rescue craft, and the New Brighton crews have undertaken many remarkable services, including several medal-winning rescues, with senior helmsman Bev Brown becoming one of the most decorated inshore lifeboat crewman in the history of the RNLI.

In its 150 years of operation, the New Brighton lifeboat station has gained a remarkable record of service with forty-eight awards for gallantry being made to the dedicated volunteers. Researching and writing about the station's history has been a privilege and I am full of admiration for the dedication and commitment shown by the lifeboat crews that undertake the work of sea rescue.

Nicholas Leach, Lichfield, December 2014

Liverpool's Early Life-savers

lthough the New Brighton lifeboat station has been operational for 150 years, and has a fine record of service, it was pre-dated in and around the Mersey by several other lifeboats, and, in fact, the area can lay claim to having the first lifeboat station in the British Isles – at Formby – long before the founding in 1824 of the Royal National Institution for the Preservation of Life from Shipwreck, the forerunner of the Royal National Lifeboat Institution (RNLI). Charts of the area from the 1770s, produced as the port of Liverpool began expanding, showed the dangers to ships entering or leaving the ever-expanding port of the numerous sandbanks around the river entrance. A chart produced by P.P. Burdett, which marked the Burbo sandbank and the Formby Channel as the main entrance into the Mersey, included several footnotes in its second edition, which was 'corrected to 1776'. One of these provides the first mention of a '[life]boat' at Formby. It reads:

> 'On the Strand about a Mile below FORMBY Lower Land Mark there is a Boat House, and a Boat kept ready to save lives from Vessels forced on Shore on that Coast, and a Guinea, or more, Reward is paid by the Corporation for every human Life that is Saved by means of this Boat.'

Further information about this 'Boat' was provided at a meeting of the Liverpool Town Council held on 5 March 1777, the minutes of which read: 'It is ordered that the boat and boat house which was formerly ordered to be built and kept at Formby in readiness to fetch any shipwrecked persons from off the banks, be repaired and kept up for that purpose'. At the Council's next meeting, nearly a month later, it was reported that 'Richard Scarisbrick of Formby, sailor, be appointed to take care of the Boat and Boat House erected and provided to be built and stationed at Formby to assist and save shipwrecked persons'. Burdett's chart and the two Council Minutes provide the earliest references to an organised coastal life-saving service.

Unfortunately, further details of this 'boat' are not documented in the minutes and it is not known if it performed any rescues or when it was removed from Formby. Although not clearly defined, the responsibilities of the Corporation seem to have encompassed implementing measures to help safeguard shipping using the port. The Corporation's backing and supervision of the 'boat', with a master employed to 'take care' of it, indicate that it was a reality and not just a proposal: the 'boat' actually placed at Formby appears to have been operational.

However, this boat seems to have operated in isolation until the early years of the nineteenth century as the costs of the war with France from 1793 and the subsequent disruption of trade seem to have prevented further lifeboats being built in Liverpool. Indeed, the continued operation of the 'Boat' at Formby during this period is questionable. No further mention of it is made until 1799, when William Brown was appointed by the Dock Committee 'to look after the boat in the room of the late Robert Whitfield, deceased, with the like allowance as enjoyed by his predecessors'. The station and boat were difficult to adequately maintain because

The historic lighthouse at Leasowe was restored during the 1990s. It was one of two lighthouses erected in 1763 by Liverpool Council's Corporation Docks Committee. When aligned, they marked the entry into the Rock Channel and then into Liverpool docks. The low light, situated a quarter of a mile out to sea, was destroyed by coastal erosion in 1769, so in 1771 a replacement was built on Bidston Hill, some distance behind the Leasowe light. The Leasowe light became the front or low light, and the alignment with the light on Bidston Hill provided a safe approach to the Mersey.

of the shifting sand dunes and the remoteness of the location well away from Formby village, meaning it was exposed and often damaged during storms, as in February 1802, when the 'Boat Shade at Formby . . . [was] reported to have been destroyed by the late tempestuous winds'. Although it was rebuilt, such problems explain why the station had a fragile existence during its first thirty years.

The next life-saving developments in the Mersey came towards the end of the eighteenth century, when further efforts to improve safety in the approaches to the Mersey involved placing lifeboats at various other locations. By 1800 Henry Greathead, of South Shields on the Tyne, was building boats designed specifically for rescuing vessels in distress, and in August 1801 the Marine Surveyor was asked by Dock Committee at Liverpool, 'to obtain the best information and particulars he can from Shields respecting the construction, expenses and management of the Boat called the Life Boat'. At the next meeting of the Committee, on 9 February 1802, the Chairman, having received the relevant details, ordered a lifeboat from Greathead, 'to be used as occasion may require in this Harbour, subject to such Regulations, Rules and Restrictions as may hereafter be determined upon'.

The boat arrived about a year later for, in March 1803, the Surveyor and Harbour Master were instructed 'to provide a proper place to the Northward of the Fort for the reception of the Life Boat'. By September 1803 a 'shade for the Life Boat' had been erected between the North Shore Coffee House and the Washing Gate Mill. At the next meeting of the Dock Committee it was reported that Jonathan Scott, Collector of Excise at Liverpool, 'had caused a Life Boat to be built in this Town which boat he was desirous of placing under the care and direction of the Dock Committee, and to have her stationed on the East Side of the River Mersey'. This lifeboat, built by Richard Bushell at his yard on the New Quay, was accepted by the Docks Committee and placed at the Liverpool station, while the Greathead lifeboat was moved from Liverpool to Hoylake, an village on the Wirral peninsula.

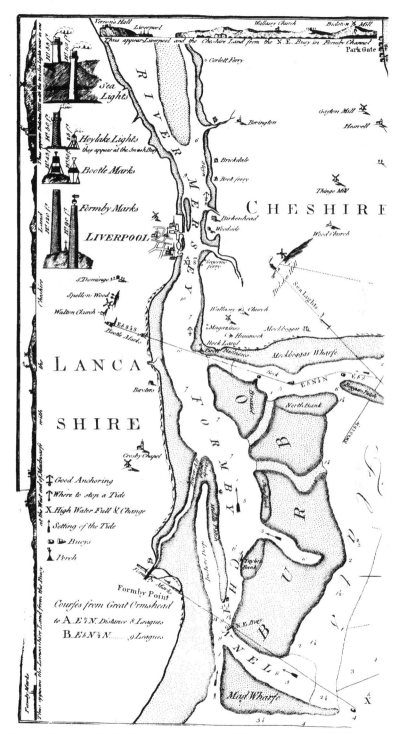

Detail of the chart by P.P. Burdett dated 1771 showing Liverpool, the Formby Channel, the Burbo Sandbank and the adjacent sandbanks, together with the main settlements in Lancashire and Cheshire, on either side of the river. Subsequent revisions, dated 1776 and 1781, recorded the existence of the lifeboat station at Formby, while the settlements at Magazines and Wallasey are relatively small. Note north is downward.

Perch Rock Fort and Lighthouse

Built in the 1820s to defend the Port of Liverpool, Fort Perch Rock is no longer needed for defensive purposes, and is instead a tourist attraction and museum. It is a Grade II listed building. The lighthouse nearby dates from the same period. (Nicholas Leach)

New Brighton has several well-known landmarks, among them the lighthouse on Perch Rock, which is situated next to Fort Perch Rock, a former defence installation built in the 1820s to defend the port. For mariners arriving in the Mersey, the lighthouse is one of the first landmarks they see. When first built, it was a wooden 'perch', hence its name, and a large post held a light on top, supported by tripod construction. It was erected on the Black Rock in 1683 by the Liverpool Corporation. When foreign ships passed the old perch, they were charged sixpence to keep it in repair, but it was washed away several times. In February 1821 the pilot boat Liver crashed into the perch and carried it away. As the cost of continually replacing it became too great, it was decided to build a new one and more permanent structure.

The foundation stone of the new lighthouse was laid on 8 June 1827 by Thomas Littledale, Mayor of Liverpool. It was designed by Mr Foster and built of marble rock from Anglesey by Tomkinson & Company, and is 90ft tall. Each piece of stone is interlocked with the next and the first 45ft of the tower is solid. A spiral staircase leads to where the keeper lived and then on to the lantern house. The revolving light cost £27,500 when it was first constructed.

Building work was only possible at low tide, and the structure was not completed until 1830. It first shone a light on 1 March 1830 which consisted of two white flashes, followed by one red, with a range of fourteen miles, and was 77ft above the half-tide level. The light last shone on 1 October 1973, having effectively been replaced by a radar system which covered the river.

Perch Rock lighthouse, seen from the sea, guards the entrance to the Mersey. (Nicholas Leach)

Efforts were made by the Dock Committee, which now had two lifeboats at its disposal, to ensure that at Hoylake was operated efficiently. It was placed under the charge of the Tide Surveyor, a Mr Marlowe, who was to 'use his best endeavours to get her Manned by Fishermen and other proper persons in the neighbourhood'. It was kept near the lower lighthouse and provided with 'a pair of wheels . . . for conveying over the sand or strand at Hoyle Lake and back again into the shade'. In 1809 the Dock Committee drew up 'Rules and Regulations to be observed respecting the Life Boat stationed at Hoyle Lake in Cheshire', and a series of rewards was to be offered to the Hoylake crews for saving lives and property. The Keeper was paid a salary of forty guineas by the Council, supplemented by 'ten pounds per annum as long as he continued and acted as Captain of the Life Boat'.

Meanwhile, in 1809 the lifeboat built in 1803 by Bushell for Jonathan Scott was moved to Formby. It had been suggested that 'a Life Boat stationed at Formby . . . might occasionally be of great advantage in rendering assistance to vessels in distress upon that part of the Coast'. A 'shade' was built for 'the reception of a Life Boat, and to be also capable of receiving a limited quantity of goods that may be recovered from any vessel wrecked on that coast'. This suggests that what had been there previously, in terms of a boathouse, no longer existed, as no one seemed to be aware of the existence of the 'boat' dating from the 1770s. Perhaps when the 'shade' was destroyed in 1802 and was never rebuilt.

The lifeboat at Hoylake, covering the Rock Channel entrance into the Mersey from the West, carried out several successful services and was probably more seaworthy than the Liverpool-built boats. But the dangers involved with life-saving were evident when, on 29 December 1810, eight out of ten of the Hoylake boat's crew were drowned after launching to the ship *Traveller*. They were all Hoylake fishermen, and had 'always displayed the greatest promptitude and alacrity in assisting vessels in distress'. The station continued in operation, however: on 2 July 1813, passengers were saved from one of the Dublin packets that had been stranded on the Hoyle Bank, and the crew were awarded ten guineas out of the Charitable Fund, 'for their prompt and successful exertions'.

The Doc Committee's three lifeboats remained in service and, in 1827, were supplemented by a fourth at Magazines, on the south bank of the river, about three-quarters of a mile upriver from the Rock lighthouse. Magazines took its name from the gunpowder stores built there in the early 1700s, close to what is now Magazine Lane and Magazine Brow. Some of the fishermen who lived there agreed to crew this lifeboat, and a boathouse was erected on land owned by Liverpool Corporation. This was completed in 1829, and was sited near the end of Magazine Lane and stood until 1939, being used in its later years by the local sailing club. The Magazines lifeboat station can be regarded as the direct forerunner of the New Brighton station, being on roughly the same site as the RNLI station.

The first lifeboat, details of which are lacking, launched on service on a number of occasions. On 17 April 1838, together with those from Hoylake and the Point of Air, it went to the aid of the ship *Athabasca*, which was aground on the East Hoyle Bank. Despite considerable efforts by all three crews, they were unable to reach the wreck and the whole of the ship's crew were lost.

In January 1839 during one of the worst storms of the century, numerous vessels were wrecked and all the lifeboats in the area were called out. On 8 January, being towed by one of the tugs from Liverpool, the Magazines lifeboat saved a number of people from the ship *Brighton*. Later that day the lifeboat went out again, this time being towed by the tug *Victoria*, and, in very heavy seas, rescued twenty-six people from the ship *St Andrews*. The following day, the lifeboat went out again and saved a number of people from the wreck of the ship *Pennsylvania*.

Later that year, a second slightly smaller boathouse was built onto the side of the Magazines boathouse to accommodate a second lifeboat, which was built by local boatbuilder Thomas Costain. Costain, at the request of the Liverpool Docks Trustees, produced a lifeboat designed specifically to meet the demands of life-saving in and around the Mersey. Costain's lifeboats were broad-beamed, not self-righting and could be sailed or rowed. They were about 30ft in length, with a beam of 9ft 3in, and rowed either ten or twelve oars, costing £180 to build. At about this time Thomas Evans, Snr, was appointed Master of the Magazines lifeboat, a position he held until the station closed.

The Magazines lifeboat rendered further services during the 1840s and 1850s. On 27 January 1840 a vessel went ashore off Formby and so the lifeboat launched, being towed out by the Isle of Man Steam Packet's steamer *Mona's Isle*. The lifeboat men rescued all twenty-six passengers and crew from the wreck, and the lifeboat went on to save ten men from the barque *Corsair*, which had run aground on Jordan's Flats.

The lifeboat was out again a year later, on 7 January 1841, when her crew rendered valuable assistance to the crew of the ship *Report*. On 30 January 1841 the lifeboat and her crew saved the schooner *Sally* and her crew after the vessel had run aground on the North Bank. Three months later, on 21 April, together with the lifeboats from Hoylake and Liverpool, the Magazines lifeboat men helped to save the brig *Mary Bell* and her crew after the brig had run aground on the East Hoyle Bank. During a severe storm on 11 February 1844, the Magazines lifeboat and her crew rescued two men and a woman from the flat *Daniel*, which was sinking off New Brighton. The lifeboat then stood by the ship *Franconia*, which had run aground on the Middle Bank, in heavy seas.

The two lifeboat houses at Magazines built in 1829 and 1839. (From an old photo supplied by R.T. McMahon/ Jeff Morris)

In 1845 the original No.1 lifeboat at Magazines was replaced by a new lifeboat, built by John Southern, of Runcorn. In 1846 this lifeboat and her crew saved the brig *Harlequin*, which was in difficulties off the North-West lightvessel. Recognition of the work of the Mersey life-savers came from the RNLI, whose Committee of Management, at a meeting on 27 November 1851, awarded Silver medals for gallantry to each of the Masters of the lifeboats belonging to the Docks Trustees, including Thomas Evans, Snr, from Magazines, who had been out on service 106 times.

By the 1850s the Magazines station only had a few more years of service as the RNLI was expanding its operations and looking to take over lifeboat services all round the country. In 1858 the Mersey Docks and Harbour Board (MDHB) took over the running of Liverpool's docks from the Liverpool Docks Trustees, and continued to run operate the five lifeboat stations.

However, the station at Magazines became superfluous in 1863 with the opening of the RNLI's station at New Brighton, and the lifeboat was therefore removed. What became of it is not known, although the lifeboats stationed at Liverpool, on the opposite side of the Mersey remained operational until the 1890s. On 14 June 1894 a resolution by the Marine Committee for the transfer of the Mersey Docks and Harbour Board's lifeboat service to the RNLI was approved, and the RNLI took over responsibility for life-saving on the Mersey with effect from 1 July 1894. On 30 June 1894 the Liverpool station was closed, without ceremony, and thus the era of independent lifeboat operation in the Mersey ended.

The penultimate Formby lifeboat, built by Costain in 1874 and replaced in 1894, was typical of Costain's design, the Liverpool type as it became known, which was used in the Mersey during the nineteenth century and was probably similar to the Magazines lifeboats.

The RNLI Establishes a Station

The independently-operated lifeboats undertook much fine rescue work, but during the second half of the nineteenth century the RNLI gradually took over the management of all lifeboat stations throughout the country and in 1862 the Institution was approached to form a station at New Brighton. Although this was somewhat of an intrusion into the Mersey Docks and Harbours Board scope of operations, Liverpool shipowners and merchants were hoping to improve lifesaving facilities in and around the Mersey. There had been little habitation and so no crew to man a boat close to the mouth of the Mersey estuary, but by the 1860s the flourishing town and resort of New Brighton had sprung up actually on the western entrance.

New Brighton had been developed during the latter half of the nineteenth century as a seaside resort serving Liverpool and Lancashire's burgeoning industrial towns. In 1830 a Liverpool merchant, James Atherton, purchased land at Rock Point, which offered views to sea and across the Mersey, and had a good beach. He developed it as a desirable residential and watering place for the gentry in a similar way to Brighton, one of the most elegant seaside resorts of the period, and hence the name New Brighton was adopted. Development began during the 1830s, with housing being built up the hillside overlooking the estuary. A pier was opened in the 1860s, and the promenade from Seacombe to New Brighton was built in the 1890s.

The river Mersey and the resort were described in 1872 by the diarist Francis Kilvert as, 'crowded with vessels of all sorts moving up and down the river, ships, barques, brigs, brigantines, schooners, cutters, colliers, tugs, steamboats, lighters, flats, everything from the huge emigrant liner steamship with four masts to the tiny sailing and rowing boat. . . At New Brighton there are beautiful sands stretching for miles along the coast and the woods were green down to the salt water's edge. The sands were covered with middle class Liverpool folks and children out for a holiday.'

During the 1850s and 1860s the RNLI was expanding its operations and soon became involved in providing a lifeboat for the Mersey. Founded in 1824 under the title National Institution for the Preservation of Life from Shipwreck, some lifeboat stations had been established around the British Isles and Ireland during the first three decades of its existence, but its success was somewhat mixed, and by the 1840s its fortunes were at a low ebb, with the task of raising sufficient funds proving difficult. However, during the 1850s a series of reforms was implemented, the service was renamed the Royal National Lifeboat Institution (RNLI) in 1854 and, under new leadership, greater revenues were generated to fund and expand the lifeboat fleet. Many new stations were founded around this time, and the establishment of the station at New Brighton was part of this expansion of the fleet.

The first moves to open a station at New Brighton were made on 27 May 1862, when a public meeting was held in Liverpool attended by the RNLI's Inspector, who was authorised to agree to the opening of a new station. A lifeboat at New Brighton would, it was argued, be able to reach wrecks sooner than either of the MDHB lifeboats at Liverpool, which were three miles further up the river, and the RNLI's offer to operate a lifeboat was accepted with enthusiasm by all present, including Thomas Evans, master of the Magazines lifeboats. He had accompanied an unusual prototype lifeboat, known as a Tubular type and named *Challenger*, on a cruise round the coast a few years earlier and was a strong advocate of this unusual type, which was similar to a catamaran. Indeed, he spoke of it with such enthusiasm that the meeting resolved no other craft would do for New Brighton.

A meeting of the RNLI's Committee of Management on 5 June 1862 concurred with the recommendation to form a station at New Brighton, and also with the boatmen's request for a Tubular type boat. As these men were to form the crew, their views were taken into account as it was common practice to accede to local preferences for lifeboat designs at this time. The Tubular type was an unusual design of which only eight were built, as it was suitable for only a few stations. New Brighton and Rhyl, in North Wales, operated them with the some success, and the type was,

'considered especially suited to the locality [the Mersey] where the lifeboats have generally to be towed by powerful steamers to wrecked vessels on the outlying banks off the entrance of the river.'

As it was planned to hoist the boat on davits at the New Brighton landing stage, launching would be possible at all states of tide. Considerations of weight were thus not as important as they were at other RNLI stations, where the boat would usually be transported on and launched from a wheeled carriage, and once afloat would usually be towed to a wreck rather than rowed.

A boat of at least 40ft length was needed, and Captain H.T. Richardson, designer of *Challenger*, was available to superintend the building of the new boat. There was some delay, however, when the local committee decided they wanted steam propulsion to be incorporated, with a paddle wheel between the tubes, but embarking on so experimental a venture was quickly discounted as inadvisable. In September 1862 John Hamilton, of the Windsor Iron Works, Garston, was authorised to proceed with the construction having quoted £230 for the boat complete, with £150 extra if steam power was added.

The boat was 'made of the best charcoal iron, and in the very best and strongest manner', while Hamilton proved to be a benevolent boatbuilder when he 'liberally gave up all profit on manufacture'. Hamilton's Ironworks was in Garston with a further Foundry at Edge Hill Liverpool. They built Clevedon Pier, Avon Bridge and much of the steelwork in Liverpool Albert Docks. Their ship's lifeboat design was selected by many companies too. The lifeboat was 40ft 3in in length, 11ft 6in in breadth, and the deck was 3ft 1in wide; the draught was about eighteen inches. She had a wood fender and an iron rudder, fourteen oars, and two masts with fore and main standing lugs and a jib. It was estimated that she could carry between seventy and eighty persons in total.

Contrary to original plans she was not suspended on davits at the end of New Brighton Landing Stage, but was kept afloat at a mooring. With her arrival at New Brighton, the lifeboat at Magazines was removed and many crew transferred to the new station, including Coxswain Thomas Evans, Snr, who already held the RNLI Silver medal for gallantry. H. Eddis was appointed honorary secretary. Provided out of RNLI funds rather than allocated to a particular donation, as was more usual, the new boat was named *Rescue* and was formally inaugurated on 24 January 1863, the day she arrived at her new station. Efforts had been to get the Board of Trade to contribute an annual grant towards the upkeep of the station, but the Board declined as they believed an additional station on the Mersey was not needed.

The involvement of the RNLI in the station's establishment was relatively minor, as the local committee and organisers were able to decide on the type lifeboat, where it was built, and what adaptations it needed for use on the Mersey. The 1 July 1863 edition of *The Lifeboat*, the RNLI's official journal, gave a good account of the opening of the station on 24 January 1863:

'A public launch of this boat took place at Liverpool . . . in the presence of a vast concourse of people, after her being drawn through the principal streets accompanied by the mayor and other authorities, military, Naval Reserve men, bands of music, under the direction of Captain H.T. Richardson, late of the Dragoon Guards, son of the inventor of this description of lifeboat.'

After the boat had become operational, a store house was built, at a cost of £31 10s 0d, in which the life-belts and other gear was kept.

Rescue served at New Brighton for the best part of fourteen years, during which time she is credited with carrying out forty effective services and the rescue of 179 lives, a creditable tally. But four days before the inauguration ceremony, a fine rescue had been performed off New Brighton in which she was not involved. During a violent thunderstorm on 20 January 1863, the American ship *John H. Elliott*, of New York, ran aground, in heavy seas. Thomas Evans, Snr, together with Thomas Evans, Jnr, William Evans and three other men, went out in a shoreboat and, with the help of the tug *United States*, rescued fifty-five people. For their outstanding gallantry, Thomas Evans, Snr, was awarded a Silver medal by the RNLI, his second, with Thomas Evans, Jnr and William Evans also receiving Silver medals.

Rescue was called out for the first time on 28 March 1863, going to the aid of the brigantine

Wasp, which had run aground on the Brazil Bank. However, the vessel refloated unaided and the lifeboat returned to her moorings. Her first effective service took place on the evening of 11 May 1863 after the brig *Levant*, of Bristol, ran aground on the North Bank in dense fog and it was feared she would break up. The lifeboat was towed out by the tug *Universe* and got as close as possible to the stranded vessel, at which point the lifeboatmen dropped anchor. They then veered down towards the casualty and, eventually, the crew of ten were rescued, while the vessel refloated on the following tide. The coxswain reported afterwards that the lifeboat towed and 'behaved well' when alongside the vessel, and the RNLI's account concluded that 'in the absence of the lifeboat, the crew of the *Levant* would have perished'.

Six weeks later, on 27 June 1863, *Rescue* was in action again, going out to the schooner *Vigilant*, of Kirkcaldy, which had run aground on Taylor's Bank at the entrance of the Mersey and was spotted in difficulties from New Brighton. The Tubular lifeboat headed out under sail and succeeded in rescuing the casualty's crew of six just minutes before it capsized and sank, becoming a total wreck. On 1 February 1864 *Rescue* went to the ship *Contest*, of Liverpool, which was into difficulties in heavy seas off New Brighton. With the help of the lifeboatmen, the ship and her crew of eighteen were taken upriver to safety. A few weeks later, on 19 April 1864, the New Brighton lifeboatmen were in action again, being called out when the barque *Corea*, of Guernsey, got into difficulties, so the boat and her two crew were brought to safety.

An engraving showing New Brighton's first lifeboat, the 42ft Tubular Rescue, which was built in 1863 and served the station until 1876.

Although good enough under sail, *Rescue* was found to be heavy under oars and, in fact, in the main too heavy to be efficient, and when the RNLI's Inspector visited the station in February 1864 he found it to be 'in a very neglected state'. So, at a meeting of the RNLI's Committee of Management on 17 May 1864, to improve the station's efficiency, it was decided to place a second lifeboat at New Brighton, a move which had the full support of the local committee. The boat supplied was conventional in design, being a 33ft ten-oared self-righter, but was built of iron rather than wood. She had been built in 1863 for the Teignmouth station in Devon, but proved unsuitable there, and so was sent to New Brighton. She was taken by railway from Devon to London, and then via the Great Western Railway, to Birkenhead, arriving on 20 July 1864.

Appropriated to a gift from Joseph Leather, a Liverpool merchant and cotton broker of Fairfield Mount, who gave the RNLI £351 3s od and who had previously given the lifeboat at Holyhead, the iron self-righter was named *Willie and Arthur* after the donor's two sons and was kept afloat in the Mersey. Three days after she arrived, on 23 July 1864, the lifeboat went afloat, with the donor on board, and was taken from Birkenhead to New Brighton where the crew were reportedly 'much pleased with the lifeboat'. Being smaller and lighter than the Tubular, she was more convenient to use for casualties in the immediate vicinity, and launched during a severe northerly gale on 28 October 1865 to the schooner *Earl of Zetland*, which ran aground on the Great Burbo Bank. In spite of very heavy seas, the lifeboatmen succeeded in refloating the vessel, which, with her crew of five, was taken safely into port.

The iron-hulled *Willie and Arthur* also proved to be unsatisfactory because keeping her afloat led to her deteriorating. A boathouse was sought by the RNLI, but a suitable site could not be obtained, and so she was replaced in April 1867 by a new, wooden-hulled 32ft by 7ft 6in self-righter, named *Lily*, having been provided from another gift received from Joseph Leather, of Liverpool. To accommodate this lifeboat, a 'commodious wooden boathouse . . . in a very good position' was built, the cost of which was met by J.C. Ewart, a Vice-Chairman of the New Brighton Branch. This boathouse was situated on the corner of Egerton Street, on land later occupied by the Tivoli Theatre. Two of the hauling-off rings, which were used to help launch the lifeboat and were set in the wall on the beach opposite, survived the eventual demolition of the boathouse. *Lily* was built by Woolfe, at a cost of £247 15s od and her launching carriage cost £83 10s od.

By the time *Lily* had taken up her duties as the No.2 lifeboat, the No.1 lifeboat *Rescue* had been taken to Hamilton's boatyard for repairs in November 1866 and it was decided to make various alterations at the same time. While she was away, the former Newbiggin lifeboat *Latimer* was placed on temporary duty. A conventional, wooden-hulled 34ft self-righter, she recorded only one rescue at New Brighton. This came on 25 February 1867, when she went to the barque *Coquimbo*, of Sunderland, which had run aground on the Jordan Flats. The lifeboat was towed out by the tug *Rover* and succeeded in getting alongside the casualty saving all fourteen members of the crew, as well as a pilot.

The renovation of the Tubular took the best part of a year; the boat was more or less completely rebuilt, emerging with a length of 42ft and breadth of 10ft, with the extensive work costing £350 12s 0d. The generous gift of Joseph Leather, allocated to the station in 1864 and originally used for the first No.2 lifeboat, was used to cover the costs of the rebuild, so the boat was given the name *Willie and Arthur* when she returned to station in August 1867. She was found to be greatly improved, and 'is reported to be much liked by the crew', with one Inspector who took her out under sail, remarking that she was 'far superior' to the Tubular boat serving at nearby Rhyl.

Being kept afloat in the river proved to be something of a hazard for the lifeboat as she was very exposed. On 25 November 1869 she was damaged at her moorings when a large part of a wrecked vessel drifted down onto her, holing her tubes in several places, so she went to Hamilton's to be repaired. Then, early in 1872, it was found that the lower parts of the tubes were getting thin because they were in contact with the water the whole time, and that the large amount of sand in the river was causing this effect. So, to improve matters it was resolved to obtain a second Tubular which would be kept on the shore, but this did not materialise until 1876.

Meanwhile, the self-righter *Lily* served as the No.2 lifeboat, staying for eleven years despite not being well liked by the crew,

A generic drawing the The Lifeboat showing the RNLI's standard self-righting lifeboat on its carriage. The self-righters at New Brighton were not liked by the crews and lasted only a few years.

who preferred the larger Tubular lifeboat which was more stable. *Lily* answered only four service calls during her time, none of which resulted in an effective service. The fact that she capsized on exercise on 2 April 1870, fortunately without loss of life, did nothing to help her gain the crew's confidence, and during a visit to the station by the Assistant Inspector in December 1874 they refused to take her out on exercise. They complained that she was 'too small and did not tow well, that she had upset once while on tow, and nearly did so again on the occasion of the Shah's visit to the Mersey'. *Lily* left the station in October 1878 to be replaced by another Tubular lifeboat.

Meanwhile, the Tubular *Willie and Arthur* continued to her work as the No.1 lifeboat, usually with tug assistance. On 26 September 1869, during a severe north-westerly gale and heavy seas, she went out to the barque *Empress*, of Prince Edward's Island, which had struck Taylor's Bank. The lifeboat was towed out by the tug *Rock* and the lifeboatmen succeeded in getting alongside the casualty to save eighteen people from the barque, including one stowaway.

Less than a month later, on 19 October 1869, she was out again after Taylor's Bank claimed another victim, the schooner *Elephant*, of Ulverston. *Willie and Arthur* put out at about 7am, and was towed to the scene by the tug *Resolute*, enabling her to approach the wreck from windward. With great skill, Coxswain Thomas got alongside and one man was rescued. The ship's master was then spotted, lashed high up in the rigging of the foremast, unable to move. Despite the fact that the schooner was rapidly breaking up, Coxswain Thomas jumped aboard and began climbing the rigging. Suddenly, the foremast gave way and crashed over the side, drowning the ship's master, with Coxswain Thomas only narrowly escaping being drowned himself. For his considerable courage in attempting to save the master, Coxswain Richard Thomas was awarded a Silver medal by the RNLI

In very heavy seas and a strong south-westerly gale the barque *Ida Maria*, of Danzig, ran aground on the Little Burbo Bank on 12 May 1870. *Willie and Arthur* put out and, following a considerable struggle against the weather, the lifeboatmen brought their boat close enough to rescue the ship's crew of fourteen. Later that year, on 28 August, this lifeboat saved the crew of five from the flat *Rattler*, of Liverpool, which had run aground on the North Bank, in heavy seas and a full gale. And on 16 November 1872 she was also called out, this time going to the aid of the local barque Vale of Nith, which ran aground on the West Middle Sands. With the help of the lifeboatmen, the barque was eventually refloated and she and her crew of twenty-one were taken safely into port.

Perhaps the most notable incident in which the Tubular was involved came on the wild night of 27 September 1875, when she was at hand following the tragic capsize of the Liverpool Tubular lifeboat. Both New Brighton and Liverpool lifeboats had gone out to help the American ship *Ellen Southard*, of Richmond, Maine, a timber ship which had been aground on Taylor's Bank at the mouth of the Mersey for most of the night, her masts fallen and her crew being repeatedly swept by the heavy seas. During the previous night 'a storm of unusual violence had raged over the greater part of these islands', according to the RNLI's official account, and at daybreak news that the vessel was aground was received, and so the lifeboatmen were summoned. The No.1 Tubular lifeboat *Willie and Arthur* slipped her moorings and was taken in tow by the steamer *Spindrift*. The Liverpool lifeboat, operated by the Mersey Docks and Harbour Board, was also launched, and she was towed by a faster steam tug, *Rattler*, so arrived on scene first.

However, the huge waves made it almost impossible for the Liverpool boat to be taken alongside but, as the lifeboat rose on one of the waves, the wife of the ship's captain jumped aboard the lifeboat and the rest of the crew were then dragged through the sea by ropes to the supposed safety of the lifeboat. Once everyone had been taken off the ship, the lifeboat set off for home, threading her way through the mass of floating wreck and timber, and to deeper and safer water.

The lifeboat's master, James Martin, ordered the foresail be set, but a huge wave was seen bearing down on the lifeboat, appearing 'like a high wall', and Martin shouted to all those on board to 'hold on'. The wave struck the lifeboat on the quarter and lifted her high into the air 'like a plaything' and, in an instant, capsizing her. On board were thirty-one people, all of whom were thrown into the sea, and found themselves 'struggling in the midst of the broken water, striving, as they rose to the surface from under the boat, to save themselves by clinging to her as she tossed about bottom up'. The master, Captain D.H. Woodworth, and his wife, who were seen to go down together as they drowned. Others, after clinging to the bottom of the upturned lifeboat for a short time, became exhausted, were washed off and drowned.

The steam tug *Rattler* was unable to help as the water was too shallow for her to get close, but the New Brighton lifeboat *Willie and Arthur*, although a considerable distance to leeward, was able to offer assistance and was quickly brought alongside the upturned boat, rescuing twenty people, twelve of whom were lifeboatmen. Of those who had been on board the lifeboat when she capsized, eleven were lost: the master, his wife, the pilot, two of the mates, and four of the seamen, together with three of the crew of the capsized lifeboat. But the remainder were saved, and *Willie and Arthur*, towed by *Rattler*, brought the eight seamen and eleven lifeboatmen safely to the shore at New Brighton.

Following this tragic incident and the efforts made by the New Brighton crew, the American Government awarded Gold Medals to each of them and to each of the survivors from the Liverpool lifeboat, with $200 ($600 in total, equalling £123 5s 9d) being awarded to each of the families of the lifeboatmen who died. A letter thanking the crew of the New Brighton lifeboat from the master of the Liverpool boat, James Martin, was later published in the local newspaper:

'I have refrained till now from expressing publicly the thanks of myself and crew of the Liverpool Dock Trustees' Tubular Lifeboat to Captain Thomas and the crew of the New Brighton Tubular Lifeboat . . . for rescuing us after our boat had capsized on Jordan Hats . . . For myself I am at a loss how to thank them, and can only assure them that their services can never be forgotten by myself, my wife, and children.'

He was particularly impressed by the speed with which the New Brighton lifeboat arrived to help, and concluded his letter by saying: 'I shall always feel, as long as the New Brighton Lifeboat is under the command of Captain Thomas and his brave crew, that we have to compete with as gallant and disciplined a crew as can be found round this or any other kingdom.'

The final two services performed by *Willie and Arthur* were to vessels that had gone aground on the sandbanks. At sunset on 17 January 1876, while inward bound and heavily laden with a general cargo, the barque *Brothers Pride*, of St John's, ran aground on Taylor's Bank, while under tow by the tug *Tartar*. With only a light breeze blowing and a slight sea, there was no immediate danger to the vessel or her crew and so the tug returned to port, to obtain some lighters, onto which it was intended to offload some of the cargo and thereby enable the barque to be refloated.

But, when the tug returned to the vessel, conditions had changed and a very strong wind was blowing with heavy seas breaking over the stranded vessel. So the tug immediately made for New Brighton and took *Willie and Arthur* in tow at 11pm. The night was very dark and cold and, as they headed out towards the stranded vessel, the tug suddenly ran aground, with the lifeboat smashing into her stern. The lifeboatmen only narrowly escaped being injured, although the lifeboat's bows were damaged. Despite this, the tow was slipped and the lifeboatmen carried on, reaching *Brothers Pride* at 2.30am. They rescued all eleven crew who, after being landed at 5am, had to be taken to hospital as they were suffering frostbite. Meanwhile, on the rising tide, *Tartar* refloated undamaged, and returned safely to port.

On 4 March 1876 the schooner *Iona*, of Belfast, while inward bound to Liverpool with a cargo of stone, ran aground on Formby Spit and quickly sank In heavy seas and a north-westerly gale, with her crew of four having to take to the rigging. *Willie and Arthur* was called out at 3.40pm and, when the lifeboatmen arrived on scene, all that could be seen of the schooner was the top portion of her mainmast, to which three men were desperately clinging, with the master having been swept away earlier and drowned. With great difficulty, Coxswain Thomas manoeuvred the lifeboat close enough to rescue the three men, who were landed at 8pm.

The second Willie and Arthur

Maintaining the station and its lifeboats was not always straightforward. It was in an exposed position, and keeping the boats moored afloat meant they were open to the elements all the time. Lifeboats at most other stations were in boathouses during this period, and keeping a boat afloat was not standard practice. Difficulties were experienced on 6 October 1873, when a very high tide caused considerable damage to the slipway and undermined the boathouse. Repairs were effected so that it would be better protected in future, but the situation was not ideal.

The Tubular boat was being repaired during this time, and so the self-righter *Lily* was being kept afloat. It was found that the bottom of the Tubular had almost no paint, although otherwise the boat was in good order. The boat was repainted immediately, and was soon operational. On 20 October 1873 the Assistant Inspector took her out on exercise in severe weather, to ensure the repairs had been carried out properly, and reported afterwards that he

'considered the Boat a very fine one. She towed better than he expected and under Canvas with leeboard down, she turned to windward well. She admitted more water than one of the Self-righting Boats would do, as it came in beneath as over all; but she was exceedingly steady in a heavy sea and would blow her masts away without heeling over much'.

He went on to say that,

'The crew had the most unbounded confidence in the boat. The men . . . thought well of the Self-righting Lifeboat for inshore work, [but] they did not think her fit to tow out to the Sandbanks and after being accustomed to a Boat so strong as the Tubular, he was not surprised at their feeling cramped in the other {boat].'

A week later, at a meeting of the Local Committee attended by the Assistance Inspector, the crew made the case to have a second Tubular lifeboat built for the station, 'to be kept in readiness in case the other was damaged'. The intention was that one of the two could be taken off service more frequently for checking leaks and repainting the iron work, which was vulnerable to the exposed conditions, and the spare boat would be kept ashore.

There was some delay in acquiring the new Tubular boat and an order was not placed until February 1876 with Hamilton's Windsor Iron Works at Garston, who had tendered £562 10s 0d to undertake the work. The plans were not delivered to Hamilton until April 1876 and by November she was largely complete. The new lifeboat, which took over the name *Willie and Arthur* and became the No.1 boat, was launched on 20 December 1876 and, like her predecessor, was also built of iron. But she was somewhat larger, measuring 45ft by 11ft, making her the largest Tubular lifeboat built. She was fitted for pulling fourteen oars and had a two-mast lugger rig like her predecessors.

By the time the new lifeboat had arrived, the old Tubular had been brought ashore and placed on a carriage on the foreshore to be held in reserve, although she was in something of a leaky condition. However, on 30 January 1877 her days were ended when she was swept from the carriage during heavy seas, and was left stranded on top of the sea wall of a nearby plantation. After much effort by the lifeboat crew, she was eventually salved, but her tubes had been very badly damaged and, having to be supported

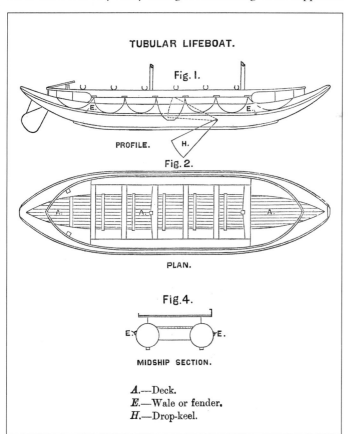

TUBULAR LIFEBOAT.

Fig. I.

PROFILE.

Fig. 2.

PLAN.

Fig. 4.

MIDSHIP SECTION.

A.—Deck.
E.—Wale or fender.
H.—Drop-keel.

A generic line drawing from The Lifeboat of a Tubular lifeboat dating from the early 1900s. Of the eight Tubular lifeboats operated by the RNLI, this depicts the last, Caroline Richardson, which served at Rhyl. New Brighton's last Tubular, Henry Richardson, left the station in 1898 after a decade of service.

by casks lashed to her sides, she was towed to Hamilton's Garston yard where it was to be ascertained what repairs were required. The carriage was also damaged in the bad weather, as was the No.2 boathouse.

Hamilton's tendered £490 to return her to a serviceable condition, but as a new boat could be built for £500 it was clear this was not worthwhile. After deliberation, the RNLI's committee of management believed the most economical way to effect repairs was to tender for a new pair of tubes, but it seems this was not done and the boat was subsequently broken up. The 1862-built *Rescue/Willie and Arthur* is credited with forty service launches and the rescue of 179 lives during almost fourteen years on station.

This new *Willie and Arthur* was soon in action, being called out at 1.30pm on 28 January 1877 to a vessel reported in distress near Taylor's Bank. The lifeboat was towed out by the tug *Hercules* and found the casualty, the sloop *Darling*, of Beaumaris, anchored in a dangerous position. Some of the lifeboatmen boarded the sloop and helped the two crew weigh anchor, after which the sloop was towed to Liverpool by the tug.

Just two days later, *Willie and Arthur* was in action again, going to the barque *I.E. Chase*, of Savannah, which got into difficulties when all her sails were blown out. Despite extremely severe conditions, with the heaviest seas the lifeboat crew had ever experienced, the lifeboat succeeded in getting alongside and some of the crew boarding the casualty, securing a tow-line to her from the tug *Guiding Star*, which then towed her safely into port. The seas were so heavy during this service that most of the lifeboat's oars and other gear were washed overboard.

Less than a month later, on 20 February 1877, *Willie and Arthur* and her crew were busy. They were called out at 1am to an Italian barque, which had been reported to be in difficulties in extremely heavy seas and a severe northerly gale. In the pitch black and intense cold of the night, and towed out by the tug *Guiding Star*, the lifeboat men reached the vessel off Crosby at 4am and helped secure a towline from the tug so the vessel could be towed to safety.

As the lifeboat returned to her moorings, another call was received when the ship *Marietta*, of Liverpool, outward bound for Bombay, went aground on the Bar. So the lifeboatmen immediately cast off again and, this time towed by the tug *Great Western*, quickly reached the casualty. The vessel had broken her back, her main and mizzen masts had been lost overboard and the crew of twenty-five could be seen clinging desperately to the fore-rigging and part of the vessel's poop, which was all that was still visible above the waves. Because the water was very shallow and considerable debris was floating in the water, Coxswain Thomas was unable to take the lifeboat alongside and so dropped anchor as close as he could before throwing a line across to the shipwrecked men. Thirteen men were hauled to safety through the foaming white water by this means of rescue, but sadly one was drowned. Six other members of the crew were rescued by the Liverpool lifeboat, while two others were swept away and drowned.

Soon after these services, an Inspector undertook a routine visit to the station and remarked that the new Tubular lifeboat was 'afloat and ready, a fine looking craft, but looks slightly hogged', meaning she was higher amidships than at bow and stern. He wondered if, when she was being launched by crane from the builder's yard, the slings had been too close together, thus allowing the tubes to sag. If this was the case her rivets were probably strained and likely to leak.

Accordingly some tests were carried out, with weights used to keep the tubes almost submerged. In sixty hours, only two of twenty-two compartments had leaked more than an inch of water, a negligible amount by iron ship standards. On a further test, one compartment leaked slightly more in four and half days and some slack rivets were found. The boat was

brought ashore and the builders tried applying water pressure to the compartments, but no serious leakage problems were revealed. A few rivets needed to be tightened, but it was concluded that the 'hog' was an optical illusion.

New Brighton lifeboat crew from the late nineteenth century. (By courtesy of New Brighton RNLI)

The RNLI's Committee of Management decided, at a meeting held on 5 June 1877, to award a Silver medal to Hiram Linaker, a member of the crew since the station opened in 1863 and who had since been out on service thirty-seven times and helped to save ninety-six lives. Recognising volunteer lifeboat crew who had given long service in this way was standard procedure during the second half of the nineteenth century.

New No.2 lifeboat

After a few month's experience with the new boat, the crew realised that she was in fact too large and heavy to be worked effectively under oars, except in very favourable conditions. The Coxswain also said that she was less buoyant than her predecessor, and shipped more water over the bows when under tow, something that had already been experienced on service. A later report went further, stating that she was unwieldy and unmanageable, her thwart layout was unsuitable, and there was not enough room in the stern sheets, but despite the criticisms the report ended by saying she was an excellent boat from the safety point of view.

However, during 1877 the New Brighton lifeboatmen began pressing for the No.2 lifeboat to be replaced by another Tubular lifeboat, especially following the discovery of the shortcomings in the 45ft second *Willie and Arthur*. With the old Tubular no longer available, having been broken up, a second, slightly smaller Tubular boat was required which, it was anticipated, would prove more useful than the No.2 lifeboat, the conventional and disliked self-righter *Lily*.

The RNLI's Committee of Management, at a meeting on 8 January 1878, agreed and a 40ft Tubular was ordered from Hamilton. To overcome the tendency of the bows to dip when towing, as had been found on the existing Tubulars, it was suggested that the tubes on the new boat should be of greater diameter forward. Flatter tops to the tubes were also considered, but abandoned when it was realised that this would reduce the buoyancy of the lee tube when the boat heeled under sail. Hamilton quoted £526, less £20 for the iron of the old Tubular. The order was confirmed in January 1878, and the boat was delivered to on 30 October. She measured 40ft by 8ft 10in, rowed twelve oars, and her sails were two standing lugs and a jib. Her cost was provided out of a gift to the RNLI from John Hay and Co, of Liverpool, and she was named *Stuart Hay*.

This lifeboat was kept afloat at moorings in the river and the old wooden boathouse was retained for use as a store until 1887, when it was demolished, after which a house in Egerton Street, No.99, was used. This house was used until 1974, when it was sold and later became a private house. During the late 1870s the RNLI Inspectors and Local Committee discussed at length the possibility of keeping the lifeboats out of the water, and proposals were put forward for building a cradle or davits on the Landing Stage to haul them clear or just hauling them onto the stage itself. But the costliness of the proposals, together with their impracticality on a number of levels, meant they were rejected.

Instead, the RNLI supplied a boarding boat so the crew could get to the moorings more easily; previously, they had used a boat kept on the Stage at the end of the pier, but this was too small to take all the crew out. So in December 1877 a small boat, measuring 24ft by 6ft 9in, was ordered from the London-based boatbuilder Woolfe & Son. Delivered to the station in July 1878, this boat was kept suspended from davits on the Ferry Landing Stage.

Once *Stuart Hay* was on station, *Willie and Arthur* was brought ashore and placed under a tarpaulin. In 1879 the old Magazines lifeboat house was leased at an annual rent of £6 and enlarged to accommodate her at a cost of £55. She remained available for service, and was used occasionally until 1888. She was given a thorough survey after being laid up, and in April 1890 was reported to be unfit and past repair, so she was sold for scrap. She had been used on service, in January 1881 and twice in 1885, but redundant for much of her time, and ended her days with a record of seventeen lives saved.

Stuart Hay served as the No.2 lifeboat for just ten years, during which time she undertook only two effective services. She was little used party because she was found to be defective in several places, including having leaks in several of her compartments, and in the two months after she had arrived on station, she had to be beached and repaired on three occasions. With Hamilton going into liquidation in November 1878, getting a reliable yard to undertake the repairs proved somewhat difficult, but early in 1880 a district inspector's report said that *Stuart Hay* had been repaired and was operational. On exercise he found her 'wonderfully stiff under canvas and very handy', and her crew liked her very much.

Her first service came in the early hours of 12 February 1880 when she went to a steamer which had gone aground on the Askew Bank. Quickly manned, *Stuart Hay* was towed out by

the tug *Rover* and found the steamship *Anatolian*, of Liverpool, in difficulty. At the Captain's request, the lifeboat stood by for several hours before transferring twenty-six of the ship's crew to the tug, which landed them safely at Liverpool.

Although her effective services were few and far between, *Stuart Hay* did launch on several other occasions without managing to complete a rescue. On 26 January 1883 she launched at 1.30am she slipped her moorings following a report that distress signals had been sighted. In a severe gale she proceeded to sea, towed by the tug *Gladiator*. For many hours the lifeboatmen searched for a casualty but could not find any vessel in need of assistance. Huge waves repeatedly swept clean over the lifeboat during the search, and two of her crew were washed overboard. One, Henry Evans, was picked up safely, but in the darkness and heavy weather there was no sign of his colleague, Charles Finlay; his body was later picked up by the crew of a passing steamer. He had been a stage-man on New Brighton Pier and his tragic death left a widow and five children. A fund was opened locally for his dependents, a total of £1,100 eventually being collected including £200 contributed by the RNLI.

The second of *Stuart Hay's* two effective services came on 5 October 1883 when she went to the ship *Nuncio*, of Yarmouth NB. Second Coxswain James Whittle, who had only been appointed to the post earlier in the year, was in command when *Stuart Hay* went out at 6pm to the ship, which had been reported aground on the Little Burbo Bank. In extremely heavy seas, it took over two hours of very hard work to manoeuvre the lifeboat close enough to be able to rescue the seventeen crew, plus the Master, his wife and

While laid up in reserve on the beach, Willie and Arthur was dislodged by heavy seas in a gale on 30 January 1877, and thrown on to the sea wall. When refloated, she was determined to be too badly damaged to be repaired economically.

Willie and Arthur after the gale in January 1877, being pushed off and into the river. (By courtesy of New Brighton RNLI)

two pilots. The survivors were transferred to a tug and the lifeboat landed the other survivors at New Brighton, where the Master and his wife, both of whom were suffering greatly from exposure, were taken to Mr Whittle's home and 'given every attention'.

On 28 January 1884 a terrible tragedy occurred on Taylor's Bank. At 2am *Stuart Hay* was towed out in response to a message from the Rock Light and found the ship *Juno*, of Liverpool, bound for Calcutta with salt, aground and surrounded by a maelstrom of surf. She stood by for ten hours, hoping for a moderation of the weather. In that time three attempts were made to get alongside the ship, but each time they were beaten back by the confused seas and conflicting currents. The Liverpool Tubular was then seen being towed to the vicinity and, utterly exhausted, the New Brighton crew made for their station for food and dry clothing.

The master of the Liverpool boat observed their movements and said afterwards that on one occasion he was so sure *Stuart Hay* had been overwhelmed in an exceptional sea that he signalled his tug to cast him off. He then made for the spot where he expected to find the New Brighton boat wrecked or capsized, but was glad to catch sight of her still making homewards under a fragment of sail. As a result of this he was himself in some difficulty and after a severe buffeting they managed to get alongside the Formby lightship, which sent a hawser to them and they hung on, in sight of the wreck and in turn waiting for a lull in the weather. Alas, this never came. The ships masts fell one by one, she began to break up and then suddenly collapsed beneath the waves. The lifeboat at once cast off and searched for boats or wreckage upon which some might have escaped, but found nothing, and nobody survived from *Juno*.

Within three months of this tragic event, the Chief Inspector came to the station and reported that *Stuart Hay* was 'completely worn out and unfit although only six years old'. She was not used again on service, but was kept on the shore in reserve while various alternative plans were tried, including a large conventional sailing lifeboat. In 1888 or soon after *Stuart Hay* was scrapped. The two services she had completed resulted in a creditable forty-seven lives being saved.

Meanwhile, in 1885 the No.1 lifeboat *Willie and Arthur* undertook what proved to be her final services. She was towed out by the steam tug *Constitution* after rockets had been seen from the Crosby Lightship, and from the Waterloo and New Brighton Coastguard Stations, on the night of 12 January 1885. The lifeboat crew found the screw steamer *Venetian*, of Liverpool, bound from Boston for Liverpool, with a general cargo and cattle, stranded near the bar. She had been forced to go to port to pass another steamer, and in doing so had been driven ashore on the Little Burbo Sand in the gale-force winds and heavy seas. At the request of the master and pilot, the lifeboat remained by the steamer until the tide rose, when she floated with the help of a tug, and proceeded to Liverpool. The master of *Venetian* wrote to the Honorary Secretary a few days later:

'Myself, officers, pilot and crew of the s.s. *Venetian* beg you to tender our sincere thanks to the coxswain and boat's crew for their prompt response to our signals on being stranded on the Burbo bank at 10pm on Sunday, the 11th instant, and for their kind voluntary behaviour in remaining by the ship all night. Enclosed please find cheque for £2 6s 6d, being half the proceeds of a contribution, including my own, collected at the pay table for your Life-boat Institution. The other half goes to the Liverpool boat fund. I am yours gratefully, W.H. Grant, Master B.S. *Venetian*.'

Willie and Arthur's final service came on 3 December 1885, when she was towed by a steam-tug to the Crosby Lightship, and found the schooner *Nathaneli*, of Cardigan, bound from Cork for Runcorn with a cargo of bones, at anchor near Tailor's Bank. She had missed stays, and had anchored to prevent being stranded on the sandbank. Two of the lifeboat crew went on board the vessel to assist the crew to slip the chain, and once this had been done a steam tug towed her to New Ferry.

Henry Richardson: the last Tubular

In 1884 a large conventional wooden-hulled sailing lifeboat came to New Brighton after the RNLI decided to try something different at the station. The boat, measuring 46ft by 11ft and built by Woolfe at a cost of £583 10s 0d, had been intended for use in the Reserve Fleet, so was sent to New Brighton on a trial basis. She left Gravesend on 16 July 1884 and was taken round the coast to New Brighton, where she arrived on 1 August, entering service as the No.3 lifeboat and being kept afloat at moorings in the river like the other lifeboats. During her time on the Mersey, she was not given a name, but on her arrival the No.1 lifeboat *Willie and Arthur* was brought ashore and placed in the old Magazines lifeboat house, which was leased by the RNLI from Liverpool Corporation at a nominal rent.

However, the New Brighton crew did not like the new self-righting lifeboat and she was never used on service. In February 1887 she was withdrawn and reallocated to Fleetwood, where she was named *Edith*, served for seven years and saved nineteen lives. But as Tubular boats were preferred at New Brighton, and with both existing Tubulars in poor condition, it

The lifeboat trials at Lowestoft

In 1892 *Henry Richardson* went via the Forth and Clyde Canal to Lowestoft, to take part in competitive sailing trials with other types of lifeboat. Although any authority was invited to take part, all the entrants were from the RNLI: 46ft Norfolk and Suffolk, 44ft Self-righting, 43ft Watson, and 43ft Tubular type lifeboats. The trials lasted from 13 February to 16 April, as there were several delays, surprising though it may seem, in waiting for sufficiently bad weather to make manoeuvres and trials worthwhile.

The first trial was launching from a steep or sloping beach into surf. This caused all of the boats more trouble than expected, but none more so than the Tubular. The heavy side-sweeping surf simply swept her off her skids and, as the local newspaper reported, 'she lay on the shingle like a couple of boilers'. Head ropes, stern ropes, setts (pushing poles) were all tried, but the fundamental difficulty was a loss of wave lifting power due to the space between the tubes. It took two hours to launch her and, the lesson learnt, she was not returned to the beach, but to moorings in the harbour. She was not designed for beach launching, as the other competitors were to a lesser or greater degree.

A few days later the steam lifeboat *Duke of Northumberland* was sent up from Harwich to take part in the trials as a supernumerary and to act as a tug for the Tubular. It is worth noting that no New Brighton men were included in the crews and, experienced as the coxswains on hand were, none could have had experience of so unusual a craft.

The results of the trials were announced in May. The four judges put the four boats in order of merit for each of the manoeuvres. As might be expected, the Tubular came last in respect of launching from and landing on a steep beach in surf, but all put her first for resistance to capsizing when aground. Of other firsts there were few: fitness for running ashore on outlying sands, and stability under canvas, both earned her firsts from two of the four judges. When the results were tabulated on a points basis (four for a first, one for a fourth, etc) the positions were as follows: Watson 188, Self-righting 150, Norfolk and Suffolk 127, Tubular 105. *Henry Richardson* came back in tow via the canal as before.

The 43ft Henry Richardson of 1888, the largest o the Tubular lifeboats, was used at the Lowestoft Sailing Lifeboat Trials of 1892. With much difficulty she was launched from the beach on the first day, but thereafter was kept at moorings. When on station, she was kept at moorings and was designed with this in mind.

was decided to build a new Tubular for the station. So the RNLI decided to ask Charles H. Beloe, the station's honorary secretary and a civil engineer by profession, to design a new boat.

Funding came from an appropriate source in the form of a legacy from Captain H.T. Richardson, lately living at Bryntryfroyd, Pwllheli, who died within a few months of the boat being ordered and left the RNLI £10,000 to pay for two Tubular lifeboats, one for Deal in Kent and the other for Pwllheli, in memory of his father and mother. Richardson had been co-designer, with his father, of the Tubular class of lifeboat, and the new lifeboat was named Henry Richardson after his late father. As Deal would be an unsuitable station for this type of boat, on appeal the Court of Chancery allowed the Institution to vary the terms of the will. So with the finances settled, and soon afterwards the design approved, in March 1888 the Naval Construction and Armament Company's tender of £625 was accepted. They went ahead quickly and on 23 August the steel-hulled Henry Richardson was towed from the yard at Barrow to her station.

Henry Richardson was 43ft overall, 12ft 6in broad over the tubes, which were 1ft 9in diameter forward, 1ft 6in aft and 3ft 3in amidships, at which point there was 5ft 4in between them. The height was 2ft 3½in to the upper side of the deck, then 1ft 3in to the upper side of the thwarts, and a further 6½in to the top of the gunwale. At the bow and stern the tubes were curved round so that they came together, 'forming one homogeneous structure instead of two separate tubes as in the former boats. This mode of construction will add materially to the buoyancy of the boat at the bow and stern,' according to The Lifeboat.

The deck was fully planked with twenty-eight relieving tubes, each of 5½in diameter. Keels of wood, 40ft long and 2ft deep, were fitted to each tube. There were two sliding keels forward and two aft, each 5ft long and 1ft 6in deep when lowered. A 4in wooden wale ran the length of both tubes. Her weight was estimated at seven tons, she rowed fourteen oars and had two masts with standing lugs as well as a jib. With the deep keels, the tubes of even depth but varying width and the planked deck, she differed significantly from her predecessors. The boat was divided into twenty-two watertight compartments, and each compartment had an access manhole to enable it to be cleaned and painted. The set-up at the station was described in The Lifeboat :

'The RNLI being determined to keep the New Brighton Lifeboat Station in the highest state of efficiency, have recently had built . . . a magnificent new steel Tubular Lifeboat. The boat arrived in the Mersey in August last, and was immediately placed on the moorings at the back of the New Brighton stage, so as to be ready for any services. The old boat is retained as a spare boat in case of an accident happening to the new one. New Brighton is, with the exception of Rhyl, the only station belonging to the Institution, where a Tubular boat is employed, and the crew at New Brighton will not use any other description of boat, which differs materially from the ordinary self-righting boats adopted by the Institution for most of their other stations.' The account concluded: 'since the Institution established a boat at this place in 1863, the total number of lives saved by its instrumentality has been about three hundred.'

During exercises and on two service calls in 1889 the crew became used to the new Tubular and expressed themselves to be perfectly satisfied with her performance. Her first successful service was on 14 January 1890, when she was towed out by the steam ferry boat Crocus to assist in saving the schooner Thomas, of Amlwch. The following year, beside rescues from two local shrimp boats, she saved twenty-five from the barque Hannah Landles, of Glasgow, which had run aground on the Little Burbo Bank on 7 December 1891. The Liverpool No.1 lifeboat, another Tubular type, also went out and the two crews found the barque being pounded by heavy seas. *Henry Richardson* got alongside and rescued most of the crew, with another two men being saved by the Liverpool lifeboat.

The last services by *Henry Richardson* were performed soon afterwards she returned from the competitive trials at Lowestoft, and just four years after she had arrived on station. During the afternoon of 19 July 1892 she was towed out to Formby Hole to the schooner *Renown*, of Wigtown. Despite the heavy seas, the lifeboat got alongside the stranded vessel and three of the lifeboatmen got aboard and helped to connect a tow-line from the tug. The anchor was raised, the tug pulled the vessel clear and towed her safely into port, with the lifeboat in attendance.

Henry Richardson was launched again that day, just before midnight, in terrible weather and eventually returned having saved twenty-nine men from 'certain death'. The fully-rigged 1,800-ton ship *Maxwell*, of Liverpool, had left the port during the morning with a full cargo of coal for San Francisco, in tow of the tug *Great Western*. By the time they reached the vicinity of the North-west lightship in the early evening, the gale had become so severe that the ship was plunging heavily, her decks full of water, and the tug was no longer in control. With great difficulty they turned back, but in crossing the bar the ship grounded and, the tide falling, freeing her proved impossible. When the hawser parted under the strain of pulling at various angles, the tug made all speed back to the river to seek help.

At New Brighton Stage the Coxswain was on watch and when the tug-master hailed the stagemen with the news of the

The last Tubular lifeboat, Henry Richardson, was built in 1888 by Naval Construction & Armaments Co Ltd at Barrow.

Henry Richardson under oars in the Mersey. She served at New Brighton for ten years and saved fifty-nine lives during that time.

casualty, he at once sent a man to collect the lifeboat crew and began getting the Tubular ready for service. Soon *Great Western* was heading back to *Maxwell* with the lifeboat in tow. By now the ship was fast and partly sunk in the sands, with seas continually breaking over her. Getting alongside was far from easy for Coxswain Martin and the lifeboat crew, but was eventually accomplished and the lifeboat rose and fell rapidly on the huge waves, which swept clean over the stranded vessel. There were many anxious minutes before all twenty-nine of the crew were transferred to safety, fortunately without mishap. The lifeboat then drifted back to the tug, which was manoeuvring to take them in tow, a difficult task but perfected by long practice. Soon lifeboat and tug were heading for the river and safety, and the survivors were landed at New Brighton.

But unseen in the darkness and noise of the night, the Liverpool No.2 lifeboat had passed the two craft as she heading for the wreck. A conventional 34ft Liverpool non-self-righter operated by the Mersey Docks and Harbour Board, she had also been launched and was towed out to *Maxwell* by the steamer *King Fisher*. They were first to reach the casualty and, in winds gusting up to 100mph, the lifeboatmen made repeated attempts to get alongside. But when a huge wave suddenly struck the lifeboat she was capsized. The crew clung desperately to the upturned boat, and then they saw the New Brighton lifeboat nearby. But unfortunately, the noise of the storm drowned their shouts for help and, as their boat was being carried away, in the inky blackness the New Brighton lifeboatmen never saw the capsized Liverpool boat, which was eventually washed ashore near the Leasowe lighthouse and of her crew of thirteen, two were drowned and a third died later in hospital.

During the 1890s the life-saving set-up at New Brighton changed, starting in April 1890 when the No.1 lifeboat *Willie and Arthur* was withdrawn, leaving the station with only one lifeboat for three years. In May 1893 the steam lifeboat *Duke of Northumberland* was sent to New Brighton. At the time she was the only steam lifeboat in existence, and was being evaluated at various stations round the coasts. Locally some dissatisfaction had been expressed about the efficiency of the lifeboat coverage in the Mersey estuary and the Liverpool Branch Committee of the RNLI had been planning to construct their own 'motive power lifeboat', which could, they believed, be powered by steam, petroleum motor or electricity. One result was that the *Duke* was retained longer than the single year at first proposed.

Another major change in the organisation of lifeboat cover for the Mersey Estuary took place on 1 July 1894. All four lifeboat stations operated by the Mersey Docks and Harbour Board were transferred to the RNLI. The stations at Formby, Hoylake, Hilbre Island and Point of Ayr were retained, but the Liverpool station at the Stage opposite New Brighton was closed and both of its lifeboats were withdrawn.

Meanwhile the days of the Tubular lifeboats were numbered. In 1897 *Henry Richardson* was deemed unfit for further service, and, withdrawn on 20 October 1898, was subsequently scrapped, having saved fifty-nine lives and taken part in fifteen service launches, but having undertaken no services since 1892. It was thought replacing her was unnecessary, but with a spare Tubular at Rhyl there was talk of bringing this boat in as a reserve. However, by then the New Brighton crew decided to have no more to do with this type of boat, and in October 1898 a large sailing lifeboat was sent to the No.2 station.

Steam Lifeboats

Providing an effective and efficient rescue service on the Mersey, as the country's second busiest port continued to expand during the late nineteenth century, was crucial and this was reflected not just in the fact that two lifeboats were based at New Brighton, but also that – from 1893 – one of them was steam powered. While the Tubulars had been well liked and proved their worth, they usually had to be towed out by steam tugs and, by the 1890s, the newly-invented steam lifeboat represented a better option. Two steam lifeboats went on to serve at New Brighton as the station became one of only a handful to operate a steam-powered craft.

Steam lifeboats were designed and built towards the end of the nineteenth century to become the RNLI's first powered lifeboats. A steam lifeboat, ready specifically for life-saving duties rather than the towage work most tugs undertook, offered many advantages over a lifeboat relying on sails, oars or a combination of the two. By the 1880s steam had been used for many years to power ships of all sizes, but doubts existed about the efficiency

Drawing of the first steam lifeboat, Duke of Northumberland, which was built in 1889 and had a highly successful life-saving career lasting more than thirty years, including a brief stint at New Brighton.

of steam-powered craft when used for life-saving, and designing and building a steam-powered lifeboat presented designers with a difficult set of challenges. However, the advantages steam power offered convinced the RNLI to go ahead with construction after a design, submitted in June 1888 by the London-based boatbuilder R. and H. Green, of Blackwall, was found to be suitable.

The prototype steam lifeboat was completed by Green in 1889 and, after being launched from her builder's yard on the Thames in the spring, made her first trial trip on 31 May 1889. She was named *Duke of Northumberland* in honour of the sixth Duke, who was President of the Institution at the time, and the fourth Duke, who had been heavily involved in improving the fortunes of the RNLI in the 1850s. The single Thornycroft compound engine with which she was fitted, with its 'patent tubulous pattern' boiler, produced 170hp and drove hydraulic pumps, which were in effect water jets. The engine drove a water-turbine, which forced water out through directional nozzles at a rate of one ton per minute, driving the boat forward at a top speed of just over nine knots.

Testing the stability of the hydraulic steam lifeboat Duke of Northumberland on 26 July 1889 at R. & H. Green's yard at Blackwall on the Thames. During this test, J.F. Green and H.T. Clarke were on board. (Supplied by Leslie Jones)

Duke of Northumberland photographed on the Mersey, circa 1893. She served at New Brighton from May 1893 to October 1897. (From the files of Grahame Farr, by courtesy of the RNLI)

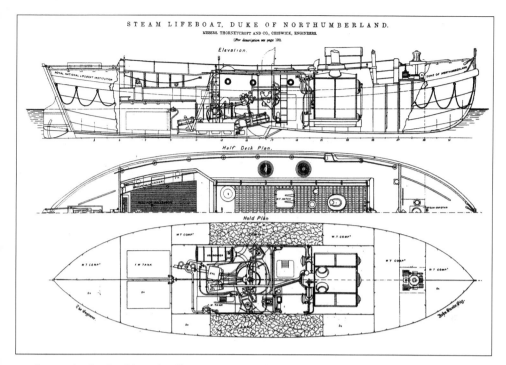

STEAM LIFEBOAT, DUKE OF NORTHUMBERLAND.
MESSRS. THORNEYCROFT AND CO., CHISWICK, ENGINEERS.
(For description see page 192.)

Elevation.

Half Deck Plan.

Hold Plan.

She was built of mild steel and was very strongly riveted, having a third more rivets than a torpedo boat of comparable size. She measured 50ft in length, had a moulded breadth of 12ft and an extreme breadth, over the wales, of 14ft 3¾in. Her extreme draught with thirty passengers, all her crew and full bunkers was 3ft 6in, in which condition her displacement was twenty-three tons. On 4 August 1890 she was taken to the Maplin measured mile for speed trials, averaging more than nine knots. With a full bunker of three tons of coal, her radius of action was 254 miles at eight and a half knots.

Duke of Northumberland soon proved that steam had many advantages over pulling and sailing. Not only were steam lifeboats able to head into the wind, they could also tow a sailing or pulling lifeboat if necessary. But drawbacks included their size, 50ft in length and more than thirty tons in weight, which restricted the number of places where they could be stationed. They had to be kept moored afloat at a time when lifeboats were kept afloat only as a last resort as anti-fouling paints were not as effective as now. Getting up the steam before setting out could take twenty minutes and even then the boats were comparatively slow, making no more than seven knots in practice despite better speeds reached during trials. Manning was also problematic as they required specialist engineers to service the boiler whilst their relatively large draught meant they were not ideal for shallow water operation. But despite the difficulties, steam lifeboats remained in RNLI service for almost three decades and are credited with saving more than 600 lives.

Elevation and deck plan of Duke of Northumberland. As the first steam lifeboat, she was described and explained in some detail in contemporary engineering magazines. (Supplied by Leslie Jones)

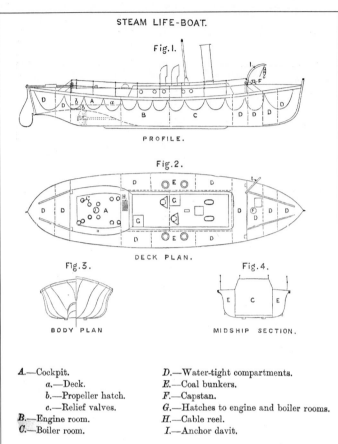

STEAM LIFE-BOAT.

Fig. 1.

PROFILE.

Fig. 2.

DECK PLAN.

Fig. 3.

BODY PLAN

Fig. 4.

MIDSHIP SECTION.

A.—Cockpit.
   a.—Deck.
   b.—Propeller hatch.
   c.—Relief valves.
B.—Engine room.
C.—Boiler room.

D.—Water-tight compartments.
E.—Coal bunkers.
F.—Capstan.
G.—Hatches to engine and boiler rooms.
H.—Cable reel.
I.—Anchor davit.

Generic line drawing of a steam lifeboat that appeared in The Lifeboat of 1 May 1909, and was reproduced in RNLI publications throughout the pre-1914 era. This shows the mast placed after the funnel, as was the case in James Stevens No.3 and two of the other six steam lifeboats that the RNLI built and operated.

During a summer running trials in and around the Thames Estuary, *Duke of Northumberland* was placed on station at Harwich in September 1890, where she spent almost two years, launching fifteen times, and saving thirty-three lives. In February 1892 she went to Lowestoft to take part in towing trials as part of the competitive trials of sailing lifeboats, spending about six weeks there being tested towing another lifeboat, passing through heavy breakers, and steaming against a tug towing a lifeboat in bad weather and a heavy sea, producing 'with most satisfactory results', according to *The Lifeboat*.

After serving at Harwich until 1892 and then at Holyhead until May 1893, *Duke of Northumberland* was transferred to New Brighton on 17 May 1893. It was the intention that she stay for a year of trials, but she ended up staying for more than four years, launching twenty-nine times and saving fourteen lives. Her first effective service came on 27 January 1894, after a vessel had been reported to be aground on Taylor's Bank. The *Duke* slipped her moorings at 9.10am, with Coxswain William Martin at the helm, and headed out into heavy seas and a south-westerly gale. The lifeboatmen found the schooner *Maria Lamb*, of Runcorn, and her crew of six, along with their dog, were rescued and landed at New Brighton.

The following year Coxswain Martin was recognised for his distinguished service at New Brighton, where he had been Coxswain since January 1892 and The RNLI's Committee of Management agreed on 12 April 1894 that he should be awarded a Silver medal in recognition of this service. Three years later, at a meeting of the same Committee on 10 January 1895, Arthur

The Wrench Series. No. 449. Printed in Saxony

Life-Boat at NEW BRIGHTON

An old postcard showing Duke of Northumberland on the Mersey with her crew on board, date unknwon. (From a Postcard supplied by John Harrop)

Simmons, who had served as full-time Chief Engineer on *Duke of Northumberland* since she was built, was also awarded a Silver medal. He had been on service with the lifeboat twenty-eight times, during which fifty-one lives had been saved.

Meanwhile, *Duke of Northumberland* continued with the work of rescue on the Mersey on 22 December 1894, when violent gales swept the country, with scores of lifeboats being called out. Nearly every lifeboat from Holyhead round to Fleetwood put out on service, including the *Duke* from New Brighton. She launched at 3.20am after signal guns had been fired from the Crosby lightvessel. The schooner *Faith*, of Beaumaris, heavily laden with coal, had gone ashore on Crosby Beach in the tremendous seas and severe north-westerly gale. With great skill, Coxswain Martin took the steam lifeboat towards the stranded vessel and, although the lifeboat struck the bottom several times during her approach, she eventually got close enough for the lifeboatmen to be able to rescue the crew of three from the schooner.

The following year the *Duke* performed two effective services, the second on 11 April 1895 to the barque *South African*, of Belfast, bound from Rio Grande for the Mersey, which stranded on Taylor's Bank in a strong westerly wind heavy seas. The vessel was seen from Formby so it was decided to send the lifeboat to her assistance. At 6.40am the lifeboat crew was summoned and five minutes later *Duke of Northumberland* left her moorings and proceeded to the scene, remaining by the ship until she refloated and was could be towed to port by a local steam tug.

Duke of Northumberland was the RNLI's first steam lifeboat, and enjoyed a life-saving career lasting more than thirty years. She is pictured in Lowestoft during the lifeboat trials held in 1892 in which she was involved. The man in the light suit and bowler hat, standing in the cockpit well is, HRH Prince of Wales.

On the afternoon of 29 July 1896 the steamer *Flying Falcon*, of Liverpool, bound there from Mostyn with a large number of passengers, stranded on the East Hoyle Sandbank near Spencer's Spit. The weather was moderate, but as the steamer was crowded with passengers it was thought advisable to launch the Hoylake lifeboat, the sailing boat *Coard William Squarey*, and *Duke of Northumberland* was also called out from New Brighton. The Hoylake boat arrived first, and arranged to transfer seventy-six of the passengers to the steam lifeboat, which was soon on scene, after which they were taken to Liverpool. The remainder of those on board the stranded steamer decided to stay until the flood tide made, when she floated off and was able to proceed on her voyage.

Duke of Northumberland was sold by the RNLI in 1923 and ended up as a derelict wreck at Ready-Mix Concrete, Terrace Road, Widnes, being mostly covered in concrete but still identifiable as a lifeboat. A sad end for an historic and unique lifeboat. (Leslie Jones)

Duke of Northumberland was called out again on the night of 9 November 1896. A telephone message from the Chief Officer of HM Coastguard at Waterloo was received stating that a vessel was showing signals of distress on Crosby Beach. The lifeboat crew found the brigantine *Emma Ives*, of Dublin, stranded with her captain wanting the assistance of a pilot and a steam tug. The lifeboat remained in attendance until the vessel was taken in tow by a steamer, after which she returned to her station.

After this service, the RNLI decided to move *Duke of Northumberland* back to Holyhead. She left New Brighton on 18 December 1897 and the following day arrived at Holyhead, where she went on to give distinguished service for more than two decades, undertaking many notable rescues. She was withdrawn from Holyhead in November 1922, and sold in 1923. Nothing is known of her location or use until, in 1994, she was found in a completely derelict condition at Ready-Mix Concrete, Terrace Road, Widnes, where she had completely deteriorated.

The steam lifeboat Queen

The usefulness of a steam-powered craft based on the Mersey had been proven by the work performed by *Duke of Northumberland*, and so plans were formulated to build a new boat for the station. A second steam lifeboat, named *City of Glasgow*, had been completed in 1894 and sent to Harwich, and another steam boat had been built for service in Australia. In planning a third steam lifeboat, the RNLI's committee discussed the matter widely and consulted the committee of the Port of Liverpool Branch and George Watson, the Institution's naval architect, before going ahead with the designs.

One of the main problems in operating a steam lifeboat was, according to *The Lifeboat*, the 'great expense of upkeep', and as a result 'many schemes were discussed to try to reduce this'. The annual upkeep of a steam lifeboat cost approximately £800, the bulk of which was used for paying the four engineers – chief engineer, assistant engineer and two firemen. So when planning a new boat it was decided to use a mixture of oil and solid fuel, a technique perfected by James Holden, locomotive superintendent of the Great Eastern Railway, rather than just coal. This, it was hoped, would reduce the number of full-time crew needed from four to, at most, three.

The station's second steam lifeboat Queen pictured undergoing trials, probably around the Thames Estuary. The boat had a 'consumption trial' on 25 August 1897, to test how much coal and coal and oil combined she consumed. Each trial lasted two hours, and on board at the time were the Chief Inspectors of the French and German lifeboat societies. (By courtesy of the RNLI)

J.I. Thornycroft & Co, of Chiswick, undertook the construction of the new boat, the hull of which was made form steel and divided into numerous watertight compartments. The boat measured 55ft by 15ft, and had a moulded depth of 5ft 6in. She was thus 5ft longer than *Duke of Northumberland* and 1ft 6in wider. Her draught on service was 2ft 9in forward, 3ft 4½in amidships, and 3ft 1½in aft; the greatest draught was amidships due to the intake which drew water into the turbine. Displacement, when fully equipped and ready for service, was about thirty-one tons.

The 200hp steam engine powered a centrifugal pump or turbine which was placed almost horizontally – similar to a modern water jet – and this gave a top speed of about nine knots. The boat's bunker capacity was three and a half tons of coal and two tons of oil. Exhaustive speed trials took place, with oil and coal both used as the fuel on different occasions to assess which was most suitable. However, in the end it was found that the power to run the air pump in the engine room, which was needed because the engine room was almost watertight, reduced the power available to drive the boat. As a result, about four years into the boat's career, coal was reverted to as the fuel, so the air pump was unnecessary.

The boat was completed in 1897 with trials undertaken throughout the summer of that year. It was decided to complete the fuel consumption tests after the boat arrived at New Brighton and so, on 8 October 1897, the boat left London for the Mersey. Basil Hall, Inspector of the Irish district, was in charge, and she was taken up the East Coast to Grangemouth, then through the Forth and Clyde Canal to Bowling, and from there down the West Coast to the Mersey. During this passage, on occasions the boat was running continuously for more than twenty-four hours. Coal was the fuel used, except for a short time between Grimsby and Berwick, when it was necessary to increase speed, and oil was tried, but not very successfully, for several hours. No heavy weather was

The steam lifeboat Queen on an early trial run with distinguished overseas visitors in 1897. For the first four years of her service, she was fitted to burn a mixture of coal and oil. (By courtesy of the RNLI)

The single-funnelled Queen on the Mersey, with her crew on deck wearing cork life-jackets. (By courtesy of the RNLI)

encountered, but the boat appears to have behaved well, and the engines performed well, which, considering the severe strain of such a long passage, and that they were new to the engineers, was, according to the RNLI's account 'highly satisfactory'.

The boat arrived at New Brighton on 27 October 1897, and the trials continued under the supervision of W.B. Cuming, the RNLI's consulting engineer. The boat had cost £4,850, of which £1,022 14s 3d was raised in Liverpool by the Port of Liverpool Branch, and £1,000 contributed by the Mersey Dock and Harbour Board, in accordance with their agreement with the RNLI. The remainder came from two legacies amounting to £1,474 17s 0d, and the RNLI's general funds. The boat was named Queen, with the agreement of the Port of Liverpool Local Committee, to honour the Diamond Jubilee of Queen Victoria, Patron of the RNLI.

On 8 December 1897 a large-scale inauguration ceremony was held at Liverpool for the new boat, during which she was formally handed over to the RNLI and the Port of Liverpool Branch by Rear-Admiral Lord Charles Beresford, and christened Queen. Following the ceremony, the Lord Mayor or Liverpool, Lord Charles Beresford, Francis Henderson and several members of the Local Committee went aboard, with Basil Hall and Coxswain William Martin at the helm, while the lifeboat conducted 'a series of manoeuvres . . . which called forth the admiration of those on board and on shore'.

Although the steam lifeboats were officially operated from the No.2 station, they performed by far the greater majority of the rescues undertaken during the first decades of the twentieth century. The first service *Queen* answered came on 25 February 1898 after the Coastguard had spotted distress rockets in the Crosby Channel. The lifeboat left her moorings at 10pm and headed out into heavy seas and a north-westerly gale. The casualty, the schooner *Robert and Elizabeth*, of Lancaster, was aground off Crosby Beach. With huge waves repeatedly sweeping the schooner, Coxswain Martin skilfully manoeuvred the lifeboat close enough to be able to rescue the crew of four, who were all completely exhausted, and they were landed at New Brighton at midnight, just two hours after the lifeboat had launched. The impressive speed with which this rescue had been effected could not have been equalled by the pulling lifeboats, even if they had had tug assistance.

During 1899 *Queen* performed a number of services, the first on 2 January 1899 when she went out in the early evening in a severe north-westerly gale and very heavy seas to the steamship *Voltaic*, which was flying signals of distress. Bound for Liverpool, the steamer had stranded on the beach near the No.8 gas buoy, so the lifeboat stood by until the vessel refloated at in the early hours of 3 January. She also went out on 11 November to the barque Falcon, saving the nine crew, and on 30 December stood by the steamships *Highland Laird*, of Liverpool, and *Albatross*.

The steam lifeboat proved to be ideal for the work undertaken in the Mersey and its extensive channels, where large vessels got into difficulty, and the majority of the rescues involved assisting stranded steamers. This was the case on 7 March 1901 after a telephone was received at both Formby and New Brighton lifeboat stations that a steamer had stranded and was in need of assistance. *Queen* left her moorings at 6.17pm, and at 7.30pm reached the steamship *Dominion*, of Liverpool, which was bound from Liverpool for Portland, Maine, with 270 persons on board. About ten minutes later the Formby lifeboat *John and Henrietta*, a 35ft Liverpool type sailing lifeboat, arrived, and both lifeboats stood by the vessel until 8.30pm, at which point she floated off the bar and was safe. The lifeboats then returned to their respective stations, with *Queen* towing the Formby boat as far as the Crosby lightvessel.

Queen and her crew performed a fine service early on the morning of 27 February 1903, going to the 2,000-ton four-masted barque *Fingal*, of Dublin, which had foundered off the North Wall, just off Gladstone Dock. In the severe westerly gale the crew took to the rigging to await rescue. *Queen* slipped her moorings at 7.18am and found the casualty with enormous seas sweeping clean over her. Coxswain Cross had considerable difficulty getting close to the barque, but, with great skill, he succeeded and the entire crew of thirty-two were rescued and landed safely at New Brighton. Performing such a rescue in difficult conditions in a pulling and sailing lifeboat would have been almost impossible.

Although the steam lifeboat was proving her worth she needed constant attention and repairs, and her full-time crew had their hands full maintaining her. Sadly, such work was not easy or straightforward, and often safety procedures were lacking. While *Queen* was undergoing repairs on 29 November 1905, two of her crew, Alan Dodd and John Jones, remained on board overnight, as night watchmen. It was bitterly cold and so they lit a fire in the stoke-hold to keep warm, then shut themselves in to try to keep heat in. Unfortunately, the next morning both were found dead, having suffocated during the night. The RNLI gave £225 to the dependents of the two lifeboatmen.

Ships were frequently getting into difficulty at Formby, at the entrance to the Mersey to the north of Liverpool, and the lifeboat at the station there was often assisted by the steam lifeboat from New Brighton. Shortly before 9pm on 12 August 1906, a telephone message was received

at New Brighton that the training brig *James J. Bibby*, of Liverpool, was ashore on Taylor's Bank. *Queen* proceeded to the scene and found the brig as reported. At the request of the brig's Captain, the steam lifeboat stood by while the Formby lifeboat *John and Henrietta*, did the same, as more than forty people were on the brig. About 1am a hawser was taken by the steam lifeboat to a tug, which was unable to get close to the brig, and by this means the casualty was successfully refloated and taken to Liverpool. A few days later letters of thanks were sent to the crews of the lifeboats, expressing the appreciation of the Committee of Management of the training vessel for the prompt help provided by the lifeboats.

During the years leading up to the First World War, *Queen* assisted one or two vessels a year on average. In 1907, on 7 August, during a moderate south-westerly gale with rough seas, she went to the schooner *Problem* of Connah's Quay, which was at anchor although not actually ashore; as the seas were so heavy the three men on board were rescued. The following year, on 2 June 1908, she went to the schooner *William Andrew*, of Garston, which was in distress off Formby having been badly damaged when in collision with a large barge. The lifeboat assisted the schooner's crew, and eventually saved them and got their vessel to safety.

Queen at her moorings on the Mersey. She is dressed overall and this could have been for her naming and inauguration ceremony in December 1897.
(By courtesy of the RNLI)

During an exceptionally severe storm on 3 December 1909 *Queen* was launched at 5.25am to go to the steamship *Bellagio*, of Glasgow, which had broken down and was at anchor close to Taylor's Bank. At the Captain's request, the lifeboat stood by throughout the day while repairs were carried out. The heavy seas and north-westerly gale made conditions on board the lifeboat difficult and uncomfortable for the crew, but once the repairs had been completed the steamer continued on her way and the lifeboat returned to station. A Letter of Thanks was sent to Coxswain Cross and his crew for this service, during which they had face very severe conditions.

Another outstanding service was performed during the early hours of 27 August 1910 during a fierce westerly gale. The Mersey Docks and Harbour Board dredger *Walter Glynn*, with a crew of sixteen, capsized in violent seas off the North Wall. Some of the crew clung to their upturned boat, while others attempted to swim ashore, with two losing their lives in the highly dangerous attempt. *Queen* was immediately called out and, as she approached the scene under the command of Coxswain William Cross, her crew could see the boat lying on its side, with several men clinging to the half-submerged superstructure.

The dredger was too close to the Wall for the lifeboat to be able to approach from leeward and so Coxswain Cross had to undertake a highly risky manoeuvre and come in on the windward side. In the heavy seas, the difficult task of getting close to the wreck was made particularly dangerous not only by the large amount of wreckage in the water but also by the dredger's funnels, her superstructure and her large dredge buckets, all of which were hazardous obstacles to the rescuers. But, after four attempts, Coxswain Cross succeeded in manoeuvring the lifeboat close enough so that the five men, who were desperately clinging to the capsized boat, could be hauled to safety.

One was seriously injured and getting him aboard the lifeboat without further injury involved considerable skill and teamwork by the lifeboatmen. After making sure there were no more men either on the wreck or in the water, Coxswain Cross headed back to New Brighton, where the five survivors were landed. For the fine seamanship and considerable courage shown during this very difficult rescue, Coxswain Cross was awarded the Thanks Inscribed on Vellum by the RNLI.

At 11.35pm on 9 June 1913, during a strong westerly gale, it was reported to Coxswain Cross that a man had swum ashore from a fishing boat and that four men aboard were in danger. The lifeboat crew promptly assembled, and *Queen* proceeded to the scene, finding the fishing boat in danger of capsizing. Three of the men were immediately rescued but for some reason the fourth man refused to leave, so the lifeboat returned to station without him. When she arrived at the stage, the Chief Officer of Coastguard advised Coxswain Cross to return as the man left on the fishing boat was in considerable danger. So the lifeboat went back, but the vessel had parted her cable and drifted up river. So the lifeboat searched for the missing vessel without result, and then returned to her moorings. It later transpired that the sole survivor had been picked up by a passing vessel and was lucky not to have been drowned.

During the First World War the New Brighton lifeboat did not perform any effective services, although *Queen* had a difficult trip on 5 December 1914. She went out at 8am to steamer *Marie Rose*, which had been reported to be in difficulties in very heavy seas and a severe north-westerly gale. But as the steamer eventually got out of trouble unaided, the lifeboat returned to her moorings, getting back at 11.40am. However, the lifeboat crew had a particularly rough trip, and one was washed overboard by a huge wave which swept clean over the lifeboat. Fortunately, he had been picked up, wet but otherwise unhurt.

Queen was next called out on 18 December 1919 after a vessel was reported to be in difficulties, but the lifeboat crew could not find any casualty and so returned to station. However, it was another very rough trip for the lifeboatmen, with huge waves repeatedly sweeping over them and their boat. Indeed, the conditions were so bad during the passage that Second Coxswain George Cross was thrown violently from one side of the boat to the other, and sustained serious damage to his kidneys. Sadly, he never fully recovered and died as a result of his injuries on 12 October 1922. The hazardous nature of lifeboat work in a relatively powerful lifeboat like *Queen*, which had virtually no crew protection, was clear.

At 10pm on 17 November 1923 *Queen* was called out in response to flares fired from the steamer *Ibis*, of Liverpool, which had run aground on the revetment in the Queen's Channel and was bumping heavily, and ended up performing two rescues. First she went alongside Ibis and rescued the crew of seven, along with a dog. And then, just as the lifeboat got clear of the wreck, flares were seen coming from the tug *Spurn*, which had also put to sea to help Ibis but had then become disabled with a rope fouling her propeller. As the tug was rolling heavily, it took considerable skill on the part of the lifeboatmen to rescue the crew of five. As one was being rescued, he fell into the sea but was quickly recovered and hauled aboard the lifeboat. However, there was a sad sequel to this service as the station's assistant secretary, W.J. Liversage, had remained on the Landing Stage while the lifeboat was at sea, suffering severe exposure during this time and as a result of which he later died.

Queen during the later years of her career, by when she had been fitted with twin funnel. She also carried auxiliary sails. (By courtesy of the RNLI)

New Brighton Life Boat.

A month later, in December 1923, with a new motor lifeboat almost ready to take up duties at the station, the steam lifeboat *Queen* took part in a spectacular rescue, which proved to be the last service she performed, when she helped to save 104 persons from the cargo steamer *Armagh* of London. The 12,000-ton steamer had stranded on a revetment in the Mersey when outward bound for New Zealand with a general cargo in moderate weather. The lifeboat went out during the evening and immediately took off the only three passengers on board a man, his wife and child, but leaving the 101 crew on board.

The lifeboat then stood by while the crew tried to refloat the vessel but Coxswain Robinson feared the ship might break her back as the tide fell. At 11pm his fears were realised, when a 15ft gap suddenly appeared in the deck of the stranded vessel. The lifeboat could not cross the revetment to get alongside the forward part because there was not enough water, so a punt was obtained from the Dock Board's tender *Vigilant*, which was standing by. Manned by three of the lifeboat crew, the punt was used to transfer all of the steamer's crew to the lifeboat in several trips. The rescued people were later transferred to *Vigilant*, which took them to the Liverpool Landing Stage.

Queen proved, during more than a quarter of a century at New Brighton, to be a very successful boat. Between October 1897 and her withdrawal in August 1923 she launched on service eighty-one times and saved 196 lives. Of the six steam lifeboats, mechanically she the best of the turbine-propelled ones, although she still suffered from serious corrosion of her inlets. After her removal from the Mersey, she was sold in 1924 and became a pilot tender in Lagos, Nigeria, working in this role for many years, until well after the end of the Second World War. What has since become of her is unknown.

Queen being loaded aboard Elder Dempster's steamer Egori in Liverpool Docks in 1926 to be taken to West Africa. When she left RNLI service in 1924, she was sold by auction for £75 to Captain J.D.H.Filbee, who intended to use her for pleasure cruises on the Mersey, but when the pier tolls were not reduced for his planned landings, he found it was not viable to operate the trips so he sold her on to Elder Dempster in 1925. The well-known shipping company made a number of alterations to her before shipping her our to Africa. She was taken to Sekondi, where it was intended that she would carry passengers to and from the shore. Sekondi was a surf port, and how long she remained in this role is not clear as the deepwater port at Takoradi was built to the west and effecively replaced Sekondi, and Queen may have moved to the new port. (By courtesy of the RNLI)

The Sailing Lifeboats

As well as the steam lifeboats, which served the No.2 station, three Watson non-self-righting sailing lifeboats were successively operated and designated the No.1 lifeboat from 1898, when the last of the Tubulars was withdrawn, until well into the motor lifeboat era. When the 1888-built Tubular *Henry Richardson* was withdrawn on 20 October 1898, she was replaced by the first of the Watson sailing craft. The new boat, which measured 43ft by 12ft 6in and was built by Henry Reynolds, of Lowestoft, cost £694 to build and, like her predecessor, was named Henry Richardson.

The new *Henry Richardson* completed just nine service during her twenty years of service. Her first effective service was on 15 October 1902, four years after she had arrived on station, and then she was only called upon because the steam lifeboat was temporarily off service at the time. In an exceptionally severe gale, the lifeboat slipped her moorings at 11.45pm to go to the

The Watson sailing lifeboat Henry Richardson with sails raised in the Mersey. She served the station from 1898 to 1919. (From an old postcard supplied by John Harrop)

Sailing Life Boat.

New Brighton.

L. Bl. & Co.

3,000-ton steamer *Heraclides*, of Liverpool, which had run aground on Taylor's Bank. Coxswain Cross took the lifeboat alongside the casualty and twenty-two members of the crew were taken off, with the remainder refusing to leave. Because of the severity of the seas, Coxswain Cross was forced to stand off the casualty but, on the falling tide, the lifeboat herself then grounded.

Meanwhile, the lifeboats from Hoylake and Formby had also launched and the Formby boat was run onto the sands, not far from *Heraclides*. Some of the Formby crew then waded across to the steamer and helped the remaining fourteen men into their boat, which landed them at 7.30am. *Henry Richardson* eventually refloated safely and returned to station at 8.30am. But, with the gale still raging, half an hour after returning to New Brighton, *Henry Richardson* was called out again, this time to the barquentine *Matador* which was aground on the Blundell Sands. The Hoylake lifeboat was also launched and both crews made considerable attempts to reach the casualty. The Hoylake crew eventually succeeded in getting close enough to save the crew of nine. For this fine rescue Hoylake Coxswain Thomas Dodd was awarded a Silver Medal by the RNLI.

Henry Richardson's last effective service came on 15 June 1918. She put to sea at 1.30pm to the aid of the ketch *E.D.J.*, of Newcastle, which had run aground and sunk in heavy seas and a near gale-force north-westerly wind. The lifeboatmen found the

The 40ft Watson sailing lifeboat Staughton, which served at New Brighton from 1919 to 1930, launching seven times on service. (By courtesy of Jeff Morris)

The 43ft Watson Anne Miles at moorings in the Mersey. Built in 1905, she had served initially at Longhope, in Orkney, and came to New Brighton in November 1930.

four crew of the ketch clinging to the boat's rigging and so they were rescued and landed at New Brighton.

On 15 October 1919 a new sailing lifeboat was supplied to the No.1 Station. She was another Watson non-self-righter, and measured 40ft by 11ft. Work on her construction had been started by the Thames Ironworks in Blackwall, London, in 1912 but when that company went out of business she had to be finished by S.E. Saunders, at Cowes. She was one of ten partially constructed lifeboats that were on the stocks in December 1912 when Thames Ironworks ceased trading She was completed in 1915, becoming the last sailing and pulling Watson lifeboat to be built, and spent her first four years as a Reserve lifeboat. Her cost of £2,279 was provided from a legacy left by the late Miss Mary Staughton, of Bedford, and the boat was christened *Staughton*.

Staughton completed just one effective service at New Brighton. On 17 July 1925 she put to sea at 11.58pm to help the yacht Lady Dorothy, of New Brighton, which had got into difficulties in the Formby Channel in rough seas and a south-westerly gale. The lifeboat stood by the yacht for some time before two of the lifeboatmen were transferred on board and helped the crew sail the yacht back to New Brighton.

Staughton was withdrawn from service in November 1930 and replaced by a second-hand lifeboat, *Anne Miles*, a 43ft Watson sailing boat which had been built in 1905 and served at Longhope (1906-26) and Howth (1926-30) before coming to New Brighton. She served the station for just six years, recording just one effective service. However, she was launched on several occasions to casualties that ended up not requiring assistance. One such occasion came on the morning of 8 April 1932 when a fishing boat was reported to be in distress in the Rock Channel. *Anne Miles* left her moorings at 11.45am in a moderate north-westerly gale and rough seas, and was towed by a tug that happened to be passing. After being towed for about half an hour the lifeboat was recalled by the Coastguard, who signalled that the two occupants of the fishing boat had been rescued by a shore boat. The lifeboat arrived back at her station at 1.20pm.

The one effective service she rendered came on 5 May 1934. She was launched during the late afternoon in rough seas and a near gale-force south-westerly wind to help the schooner *Duchess*, of Dublin. *Anne Miles* reached the casualty first, but was swept past the schooner and had to beat to windward to try to get back to help. As she did so, the tug *Yorkgarth* arrived on scene and her crew launched a small boat, manned by two crew, who then tried to reach the schooner.

However, they too were swept past and began heading towards Taylor's Bank. On seeing this, Coxswain Jones realised that the small boat could capsize at any moment and so, as the Hoylake motor lifeboat was approaching the schooner, he decided to go to help the men in the small boat. They were rescued and *Anne Miles* headed back up the Crosby Channel, where she was taken in tow by *Yorkgarth* back to New Brighton, arriving there at 9pm. Meanwhile, the Hoylake lifeboat had got alongside the schooner and rescued the crew of three men.

On 9 November 1936 *Anne Miles* was withdrawn from service and, until a new lifeboat was ready, the former Southend lifeboat *Charlie Medland*, another 43ft Watson class boat, was placed on duty. She had been built in 1904 for Mumbles, where she served with distinction for almost two decades, but was never called out on service while on the Mersey and was something of a stop-gap measure for New Brighton. She was essentially a back-up to the motor lifeboat *William and Kate Johnston*, but somewhat strangely was designated the No.1 lifeboat.

William and Kate Johnston

The importance of the New Brighton station was demonstrated when, in the May 1920 edition of The Lifeboat, the RNLI was announced that a new type of motor lifeboat was to go to the station to cover the port of Liverpool. The new boat was a new and ground-breaking design with twin engines and twin propellers among other innovative equipment. The first lifeboat to be built with twin engines, she was something of a revolutionary craft. Funding for the new boat came from various sources, but the Port of Liverpool Branch of the RNLI had been busy and raised £7,500 towards the cost by 1920, even before construction work had begun.

The Consulting Naval Architect to the RNLI, James Barnett, had designed the new lifeboat, which was 60ft in length, 15ft in

The 60ft Barnett William and Kate Johnston was the first motor lifeboat to serve at New Brighton, and the first RNLI motor lifeboat with twin engines and twin screws. (By courtesy of RNLI)

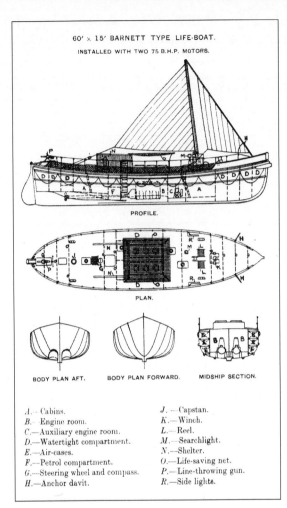

60' × 15' BARNETT TYPE LIFE-BOAT.

INSTALLED WITH TWO 75 B.H.P. MOTORS.

PROFILE.

PLAN.

BODY PLAN AFT. BODY PLAN FORWARD. MIDSHIP SECTION.

A.— Cabins.	*J.*— Capstan.
B.— Engine room.	*K.*— Winch.
C.— Auxiliary engine room.	*L.*— Reel.
D.— Watertight compartment.	*M.*— Searchlight.
E.— Air-cases.	*N.*— Shelter.
F.— Petrol compartment.	*O.*— Life-saving net.
G.— Steering wheel and compass.	*P.*— Line-throwing gun.
H.— Anchor davit.	*R.*— Side lights.

A generic RNLI line drawing showing William and Kate Johnston, the first 60ft Barnett, with full rigging and jumping net. This diagram appeared in several editions of The Lifeboat. The jumping net was later removed and twin funnels, located aft of the wheel, were added for the exhaust.

breadth, and had a draught of 4ft 6in, and was seen as a radical departure from previous lifeboat designs. The first boat of a class of four had been laid down in 1922 at the Cowes boatyard of J.S. White, and she was launched at Cowes in 1923. With a displacement of forty tons, such a lifeboat had never before been built. Her size, however impressive it was, proved to be something of a drawback because it meant that she was limited to operating from stations where she could be kept afloat, but New Brighton, where the lifeboats had always been kept afloat, was ideal for such a craft.

Incorporated in the boat's design was shelter for the crew, with the engine controls and engine room hatches all mounted at deck level. Another innovation was the level of crew protection: two cabins were provided, one fore and one aft, and these could hold about fifty people between them. In rough weather 130 persons could be taken on board, and as many as 200 in fine weather. A deck shelter for the mechanic was provided, and this covered the entrance to the engine room. The introduction of such shelters was another novel feature, as hitherto crews had been expected to cope with anything the sea threw at them more or less unprotected, which in the sailing and pulling lifeboats of the previous century had not involved going head to sea and wind, something the motor lifeboat could accomplish. Barnett considered this shelter useful as it 'also affords considerable protection to the coxswain and other members of the crew stationed aft'.

The hull was constructed of teak, double-skinned, with eleven transverse and three longitudinal steel bulkheads, which formed fifteen main watertight compartments. The idea of having two engines, in completely separate and watertight engine rooms, meant that only a jury rig was provided, consisting of a small triangular fore-lug and jib, which could be set on a single mast. Motor lifeboats with single engines had been provided with a full set of sails in case of engine failure, but twin engines provided additional

Labels within the illustration:
Compressed-Air-driven WINCH
Electric SEARCHLIGHT
FORE PASSENGER CABIN
STOVE
JUMPING NET
Boiler Cabin
AIR COMPRESSOR
Auxiliary B.H.R. MOTOR
Position of DYNAMO
Hatch to PETROL TANKS
Compressed-Air-driven CAPSTAN
LINE-THROWING GUN Once 160 yards
Hatch to AFTER PASSENGER CABIN
Starboard 40 B.H.R. MOTOR
PUMP
TWIN PROPELLERS in Protective Tunnels
X.X. WATERTIGHT BULKHEADS, 11 in all
Y.Y. LONGITUDINAL Ditto, 3 in all
Z.Z. BUOYANCY AIR CASES flanking Cabins 100 in all, in 3 tiers rendering Boat practically unsinkable

A cutaway drawing of William and Kate Johnston which appeared in the May 1922 edition of The Lifeboat. It was taken from a painting by S.W. Clatworthy and provides an idea of how the interior of the boat was laid out and published adjacent to an article entitled 'A New Type of Motor Lifeboat' written by Captain Howard F.J. Rowley, the Chief Inspector of Lifeboats. Among the new features incorporated in the boat were a searchlight, a life-saving net and a line-throwing gun. The boat had flush decks, without sunken wells or cockpits, and was fitted with a stove and lavatory so that, as The Lifeboat explained: 'for the first time, it will be possible to give at once to the rescued . . . shelter, warmth and warm food', clearly something of a novelty.

The naming ceremony of William and Kate Johnston was hald at Liverpool on 24 Septemer 1924 with Mrs Johnsyon, wife of donor Stewart Johnston, releasing the champagne over the boat's bows. (By courtesy of the RNLI)

insurance against this eventuality. Although not self-righting, the hull was considered unsinkable, a description given to lifeboat designs from before 1800 but which was perhaps something of an exaggeration. But suffice to say, she was as near to unsinkable as the skills of her time permitted, and no expense was spared.

The engines and machinery installations were of a completely new type, specially designed by the RNLI's technical staff, headed by Mr A.F. Evans. These comprised twin DE six-cylinder engines, built by the Weyburn Engineering Co, with a 5.5-inch bore, and seven-inch stroke. Each engine developed 80bhp at a rated speed of 800rpm, driving propellers of 25-inch diameter and 23-inch pitch. The Chief Inspector of Lifeboats, Captain F.J. Rowley, CBE, RN, saw the great value of the new design of engine not so much in the increased speed, which was only about a knot, or even in the increased horsepower, but 'in the very great reserve of power, enabling the Lifeboat to maintain her maximum speed under conditions of weather which would materially reduce the speed of any other Motor Lifeboat'. The engine, at full speed, developed 786 revolutions per minute and the boat achieved a speed of nine and a half knots. At this rate 120 pints of petrol were consumed an hour, and the boat had a radius of 102 nautical miles.

The launch of the new boat in 1923 was heralded in *The Graphic* newspaper as, 'The outstanding event in connection with the lifeboat fleet this year [1923]', and she was described as 'the most powerful lifeboat, not only in this country, but in the world'. The boat's harbour trials took place at Cowes on 10 August 1923, after which she toured the British Isles, travelling 2,000 miles in just over two months, going first up the East Coast and then round the northern tip of Scotland under her own power. She called at Douglas (IOM), Belfast, Dun Laoghaire, Padstow and Bristol on

William and Kate Johnston, leading the line-up of lifeboats on the river Thames in 1924 to celebrate the centenary of the RNLI. The foreign lifeboats were also in attendance, participating in the first International Lifeboat Conference.

William and Kate Johnson alongside the New Brighton Landing Stage on 28 August 1924. (By courtesy of New Brighton RNLI)

A demonstration of William and Kate Johnson's jumping net. This feature, seen as innovative when the boat was built, was later removed. (By courtesy of the RNLI)

William and Kate Johnson alongside a pier during her journey round the coast. She travelled extensively after being built, both on show and to London for the RNLI's centenary events. (From an old postcard supplied by John Harrop)

On board William and Kate Johnsonon 16 September 1924, just over a week before her naming ceremony. (By courtesy of New Brighton RNLI)

The donors of William and Kate Johnson, Mr Stewart Johnston and Mrs W.H. Kendall, on board the lifeboat with the crew for the naming ceremony on 24 September 1924. (By courtesy of New Brighton RNLI)

her way south, before heading back up the Welsh coast and to the Mersey to take up her station duties.

At New Brighton, 'a station for which she is especially suited, because of the great volume of traffic, the outlying sandbanks to the Mersey, the strong tides and the long distances which frequently have to be travelled', according to *The Lifeboat*, her services were much in demand and, it turned out, she was the busiest of any of the four 60ft Barnetts which the RNLI built during the 1920s. The others were stationed at Aberdeen, Plymouth and Padstow.

The new lifeboat's time at New Brighton was interrupted in 1924 when she was temporarily taken off station in June to go to London, where, on 30 June, together with lifeboats from five other countries, she took part in the celebrations on the Thames, to mark the centenary of the RNLI's founding. There was high acclaim from all quarters when the new boat was exhibited in London at the first International Lifeboat Conference in July for the lifeboat societies of the world to admire.

Following her time in London and with the centenary celebrations over, *William and Kate Johnston* returned north and back to the Mersey to take up her duties full time. Originally she was designated as the No.2 lifeboat, but from 1938 became the No.1 lifeboat. Her inaugural ceremony took place on 24 September 1924, at the Prince's Landing Stage, Liverpool, where

William and Kate Johnson dressed overall with her crew hailing one of the steam tugs on the river. (By courtesy of the RNLI)

she was named by Mrs Stewart Johnston. The boat, built at a cost of £16,084, had been provided out of gifts from Mr Stewart Johnston and his sister, Mrs W.H. Kendall, of Liverpool, and the name honoured their parents. Mr and Mrs Johnston were owners of the Johnston Shipping Line, which operated mainly between the eastern Mediterranean and the UK, their ships carrying cargoes which included Cleopatra's Needle, which they brought to London. Their gift had been supplemented by money raised by the Liverpool Motor Lifeboat Fund, organised by the city's very active fund-raising branches, and so it was appropriate that she should be stationed close to the city from which the funds for her building had come.

Somewhat unusually two full-time motor mechanics were appointed: Ralph Scott became First Mechanic and R. Millmore the Second Mechanic. Herbert Harrison took over from Millmore in April 1924, but unfortunately Harrison's time in service was cut short through a tragic accident. On 9 March 1925 he went out with Scott in the small motor boarding boat to carry out routine work on *William and Kate Johnston*, when the engine of the boarding boat suddenly stopped. The boat was swept three miles downriver by the strong flood tide and the two mechanics could were powerless to prevent this. A tug came to their assistance and her crew threw a line across, which was made fast. But, as the tug towed the small boat towards the shore, it capsized in the choppy

William and Kate Johnson in the Mersey, lying at her moorings. The end of the pier, where the boarding boat was kept, is just visible behind the bow, with the New Brighton Tower Building behind the boat. The New Brighton Tower, built in 1896-1900, was the tallest building in the country when completed. It was dismantled between 1919 and 1921 after falling into disrepair. The brick portion, seen here, comprising the Ballroom and Theatre remained, together with the turrets. During the Second World War the basement was used as a communal air-raid shelter. (By courtesy of John Harrop)

water. Scott was rescued, exhausted but alive, by the crew of the tug, but sadly Herbert Harrison was drowned. Wilfred Garbutt succeeded him as Second Mechanic.

William and Kate Johnston answered her first service call at New Brighton on 15 April 1925, going out at 8.40am to help the Dock Board's *Hopper No.9*, which had run aground in the Rock Channel. In heavy seas and a severe north-westerly gale, the lifeboat stood by while attempts were made to refloat the vessel. When these failed, the lifeboat returned to her moorings. On 26 September 1925 she went to the motor vessel *Innisinver*, of London, which was in difficulty while on passage from Cork, having engine problems when at the mouth of the Mersey. In the early hours, the lifeboat crew took off the vessel's five crew, and the vessel itself was eventually brought in by Dock Board steamers.

Stranded steamers were the most common casualties to which *William and Kate Johnston* launched, and the incident on 30 November 1927 involving the 10,000-ton steamer *Loch Monar* ran aground on the revetment was typical. The lifeboat slipped her moorings at 4.35am once news of the steamer's plight was known, and headed out into choppy seas and a fresh northerly wind, to help. The lifeboat went alongside and took off twenty-eight members of the crew and put them aboard a tug. She was taken alongside the stranded vessel again, and took off the remaining forty-one crew, as well as five passengers, who were also transferred to the tug, which landed them at Liverpool. The lifeboat stood by the steamer while several other tugs tried to pull her clear, but without success, and the steamer eventually broke her back.

The following year *William and Kate Johnston* went to another cargo vessel, the oil tanker *Varand*, of London, which was fully laden with benzine when she got into difficulty in mid-Atlantic;

The lifeboat medallists of 1928-29 in London for the RNLI's Annual General Meeting on 17 April 1929. The Emile Delmas rescue by the New Brighton crew was described as the 'finest service' of the year. The New Brighton medal winners were joined by the year's other medal recipients in this photo, which shows, left to right, Coxswain George Robinson, Second Coxswain J.R. Nicholason and Mechanic Ralph Scott; Second Coxswain James Sim, of Fraserburgh, who received the Silver medal; Coxswain W.J. Baker and Mr J. Atkinson, Master of the tug, of Padstow; and High MacKay, of Hilton, Ross-shire, who was awarded the Bronze medal for a shore-boat rescue.

she struck a submerged object which damaged her propeller and rudder, putting them out of action. The tanker was taken in tow by another ship and brought to the Mersey, but as the vessels arrived in the river on 17 February 1928 they were caught in a terrible storm. In absolutely appalling conditions, the crippled steamer ran aground on the Bar, so *William and Kate Johnston* was called out, putting to sea at 6.15am. Coxswain Robinson had great difficulty getting alongside the stranded vessel, with the lifeboat being damaged in the attempt to get her into position. But eventually twenty-four members of the tanker's crew were taken off by the lifeboat. An hour later, the remaining members of the crew, eighteen in number, signalled that they wished to leave the ship, so the lifeboat went back alongside and rescued the men.

The Emile Delmas service

Later that year, *William and Kate Johnston* took part in a truly outstanding rescue. At 7am on 24 November the steamer *Emile Delmas*, of La Rochelle, began dragging her anchors, four miles north-west of the Bar lightvessel in violent seas and a severe north-westerly gale, which was gusting up to 100mph. The lifeboat put to sea at 7.45am, manned by crew of eight including Motor Mechanic Ralph Scott who was on board despite the fact that he was waiting to go into hospital for a major operation.

When the lifeboat reached the casualty, Coxswain George Robinson was faced with an extremely difficult task, as the steamer was yawing wildly in the mountainous seas. It took superb seamanship and tremendous courage on the Coxswain's part to get the lifeboat alongside the stricken ship. Outstanding cooperation and teamwork was shown by the lifeboatmen throughout, especially the two Motor Mechanics working at the engine controls, without whose efforts the Coxswain could not have got the lifeboat into position. But he succeeded in taking the lifeboat alongside and twenty-three members of the crew climbed down ladders and were then dragged to safety by the lifeboat crew, or they jumped into the special net which was rigged amidships aboard the lifeboat. The Captain of *Emile Delmas* refused to leave, until his ship ran aground and then he too was rescued.

The lifeboat was damaged during this service, but Coxswain Robinson was able to bring her clear and set course for home. Conditions were truly appalling during the return passage, and one huge wave swept right over the lifeboat, washing two of her crew and the Chief Engineer of the steamer overboard. The huge wave also flooded the lifeboat's engine rooms and only with very great difficulty in the violent seas was Coxswain Robinson able to turn the lifeboat round. The two lifeboatmen, Bowman George Carmody and crew member Samuel Jones, were picked up but, sadly, they were unable to reach the steamer's Chief Engineer, who drowned. The lifeboat limped slowly back to New Brighton, which was reached having been at sea for six hours to complete a remarkable rescue.

For his truly outstanding seamanship and very great courage, Coxswain George Robinson was awarded the Silver medal by the RNLI. For their tremendous skill and courage during this most demanding service, the each of the other members of the crew were awarded Bronze medals. They were Second Coxswain John Nicholson, Bowman George Carmody, First Mechanic Ralph Scott, Second Mechanic Wilfred Garbutt and lifeboatmen Samuel Jones, John Moore and William Liversage. The owners of *Emile Delmas* later made a special gift of 10,000 francs to the lifeboat crew and the French Government awarded Gold medals to Coxswain Robinson and to the two lifeboatmen who had been washed overboard, George Carmody and Samuel Jones.

The boarding boat was used to effect rescues from time to time, and proved to be a useful rescue tool on 1 August 1932. A few minutes before 11pm that day, flares were seen by the Coastguard from a vessel near the No.7 Rock Buoy. The boarding boat was manned by the Second Coxswain and Chief Motor Mechanic, and they found the motor launch *Forester*, of Liverpool, which had run out of petrol and was drifting. The weather being calm, the launch was taken in tow to the New Brighton landing stage.

All the services undertaken by *William and Kate Johnston* in 1933 were to help local fishing boats. During the evening of 1 April 1933 the motor mechanic received a telephone message reporting that six men were stranded on Burbo Bank in a moderate north-westerly wind and rough seas. The lifeboat left her moorings at 9.44pm, and, after the crew had searched for two hours using the searchlights, two men were found drifting in a waterlogged boat. They were taken on board the lifeboat and told the coxswain that four other men were still missing, so the search continued. Eventually a flare was seen in the direction of the north bank, where the lifeboat crew found the fishing boat *Eagle*, of Bootle, with the four men on board. The boat was leaking, her rudder had been lost, and her sails were torn. The men were taken off and *Eagle* was towed back to New Brighton, which was reached at 12.45am the following day.

On 6 August 1933 the fishing boat *Madge* went aground near the Battery Rocks in rough seas with a strong tide running, and *William and Kate Johnston* left her moorings soon after 11.30pm to help. On reaching the rocks she found the boat whose two crew were taken about the lifeboat, which returned to her station. A few minutes later another boat was

reported in difficulties and the lifeboat put out again. This time she found the Liverpool fishing boat *Bonny Breeze* in danger of being swept against the seawall west of the Battery Rocks. The boat was towed to a safe anchorage and the lifeboat returned to her moorings at 1.30am.

During the mid-1930s *William and Kate Johnston* performed several fairly routine services, with her busiest year being 1935. On 25 January 1935 she went to the Pilot Vessel No.2, named *Walter J. Chambers*, which was in difficulty in a north-westerly gale and rough seas. The lifeboat escorted the pilot vessel while it was towed back to port by a steam tug. On 27 July he lifeboat she went to the converted ship's boat *Collingwood*, with four men and a boy on board, who needed help after their engine had been swamped. Getting a tow line to the casualty from the lifeboat proved very difficult, but once this had been done the boat was towed back to New Brighton stage.

The longest service of the year came on 19 October 1935, when *William and Kate Johnston* launched just after midday to the steamship *Inga 1*, of Bergen, in a north-westerly gale and very heavy seas. The steamer was dragging her anchors near Crosby, and the lifeboat stood by while a tug and the Harbour Board's vessel *Vigilant* arrived on scene. Attempts to rig a tow failed in the heavy seas, so the lifeboat stood by as the captain did not want to abandon his ship. With the falling tide, the lifeboat was forced

William and Kate Johnston approaching New Brighton pier in a heavy swell after rescuing the crews of the casualties Progress and Loch Ranza Castle on 23 November 1938. (By courtesy of the RNLI)

to stand off, and eventually left the scene, returning to station at 6.50pm, while *Inga I* went aground on the sands. The steamer was towed off the following day by tugs, while the lifeboat crew received larger monetary rewards than usual for what had been a long and arduous service.

Another medal-winning service

In 1938 *William and Kate Johnston* was redesignated as the No.1 lifeboat at New Brighton, but she continued the task of rescue uninterrupted, and performed a remarkable rescue towards the end of the year. Her last service as the No.2 lifeboat came on 15 January 1938, when she searched for a vessel reportedly in distress five miles north-west of the Bar Buoy. In gale force winds and very rough seas, the lifeboat put out at 6.40pm, and searched round the Bar Lightvessel and Buoys but could find no trace of the distressed vessel.

A wireless message was then received stating that the casualty was about sixteen miles from the Formby lightvessel, but as the lifeboat continued the search, at 1.10am on 16 January, another wireless message was sent to the lifeboat saying that the reported casualty had reached port. So the lifeboat returned to her station, reaching New Brighton at 4.50am after over ten hours at sea in extremely bad conditions. An increase in the usual monetary award

A dramatic photo showing the lifeboat crew landing survivors from the fishing boat Progress and the schooner Loch Ranza Castle, 23 November 1938. The lifeboat had been driven right over the wreck to rescue the crew, who were in the rigging. (By courtesy of the RNLI)

was granted to each of the crew for this difficult and ultimately fruitless launch.

During the summer, the reserve lifeboat *City of Bradford I* (ON.680) was on station, and performed one rescue, on 10 June, saving four from the schooner *Minnie*, whose engine had broken down and engine room flooded. *William and Kate Johnston* returned later in the year, and in November was called out for what proved to be another outstanding rescue. On 23 November 1938 the severest gales for ten years was blowing, and ships were in difficulties all round the coast. Twenty-seven lifeboats were called out on service that day, and saved a total of thirty-six lives. Several medal-winning services were performed, with that at New Brighton proving to be the most notable.

William and Kate Johnston coming alongside the Landing Stage, with three compartments flooded, bringing to safety two crews saved during the 'Great Gale' of 23 November 1938. The lifeboat was badly damaged when the coxswain took her over a sunken wreck to effect the rescue. (By courtesy of the RNLI)

The rescue began at 9.15am when that lifeboat crew were alerted to a fishing boat in distress north-east of the Crosby Lightvessel. Within eight minutes of the maroons being fired, *William and Kate Johnston* had slipped her moorings with Coxswain William Jones in command. Conditions were truly appalling, with frequent very

The damage sustained by William and Kate Johnston during the service to the fishing boat Progress and the schooner Lochranza Castle on 23 November 1938. (By courtesy of RNLI)

heavy squalls of rain and hail, and winds gusting up to 108mph. Coxswain Jones and his crew approached the casualty, *Progress*, of Hoylake, which had three crew on board, just over an hour after launching. She was labouring heavily in the conditions, but as the lifeboat reached the scene the crew spotted the schooner *Loch Ranza Castle*, of Annalong, which had a crew of four, was heavily laden with stone, and was drifting helplessly with her sails torn to shreds.

Coxswain Jones had to decide which vessel to help first. As the fishing boat was the smaller and was at anchor in deeper water, he decided to go to her assistance first. So with great skill, he manoeuvred the heaving, pitching lifeboat alongside and, after several attempts, the crew of three were rescued. A few minutes later, the fishing boat sank. Jones then swung the lifeboat round towards the schooner. Conditions had worsened, with enormous seas and violent squalls causing clouds of spray and making it extremely difficult to see beyond the bows of the lifeboat.

The schooner was already very close to the shore, right among the breakers and her crew had been forced to climb into the rigging, as their boat sank lower and lower into the waves. Coxswain Jones took the lifeboat towards the schooner, with the lifeboatmen taking soundings as they got closer, and got the lifeboat to within 200 yards of the casualty. He then dropped anchor, and the lifeboat was veered down, bow first, towards the schooner.

With outstanding skill and considerable courage, Coxswain Jones took the lifeboat closer and closer, through a mass of white, churning water. The Coxswain and the two Motor Mechanics had to work closely together during this operation, with Coxswain Jones struggling to maintain control of the lifeboat in the treacherous conditions. To reach the men in the schooner's rigging, the Coxswain had to drive the lifeboat over the deck of the vessel, which had sunk. It took two attempts to save two of the men from the vessel's starboard rigging, leaving the other two in the rigging on the port side. But as one of them managed to climb up and over to the starboard side, he too was dragged aboard the lifeboat. He immediately told Coxswain Jones that the last man, still in the port rigging, was too exhausted to move and the Coxswain realised that by now the situation was desperate.

Coxswain Jones' only chance to save the last man was to take the lifeboat round the schooner's bows and come in under her port rigging. The rescue of the three men had taken an hour and, although the tide had eased, the schooner was rapidly breaking up with none of the deck fittings, not even the gunwale, showing, and yards and rigging falling from the masts. The second anchor cable of the lifeboat was bent onto the cable by which the lifeboat was already anchored, so as to enable her to be taken round the bows of the schooner, and the Coxswain veered her down stern first, passed under the bowsprit of the wreck, and, with the help of the engines, got alongside the port rigging. The man by now was barely conscious and was incapable of helping himself. But the Coxswain kept the boat alongside the boat's rigging and, with great difficulty, the crew succeeded in getting the half conscious man into the lifeboat, where he was immediately attended to and given first aid by Second Mechanic John Mason.

The coxswain then manoeuvred the lifeboat into deeper water, cut the cable, and made for the New Brighton landing stage, where the lifeboat arrived at 12.53pm. The lifeboat had suffered serious damage while going over the deck of the schooner: her two forward compartments and the cabin were flooded, and she was down at the bows by about three feet. However, they reached the Landing Stage safely where all the rescued men were put ashore, a feat which itself required great boathandling skills by the Coxswain. The lifeboat was then taken straight to a boatyard in Birkenhead, where she was hauled out. Apart from considerable damage to the fittings, the boat was found to have three holes in her hull, the largest of which was three feet

long. Although this damage turned out to be quite serious, it had not impaired her seaworthiness.

For his truly outstanding seamanship, skill and tremendous courage, Coxswain Jones was awarded a Silver medal by the RNLI for the great skill and courage that they too had shown throughout this service; Bronze medals were awarded to Second Coxswain John Nicholson, First Mechanic Wilfred Garbutt and Second Mechanic John Mason. The Thanks Inscribed on Vellum were accorded to each of the other members of that very gallant crew, Bowman W.S. Jones and lifeboatmen James Stonall, Harry Stonall and William Douglas. Sadly, a few days after taking part in this service James Stonall collapsed and died while out fishing. This also proved to be the last service by Coxswain William Jones, who retired at the end of December 1938.

The 41ft Watson motor lifeboat Edmund and Mary Robinson served at New Brighton as the No.2 lifeboat from 1938 to 1950. She was powered by twin 35hp Weyburn engines, which gave her a top speed of 7.89 knots when built, and a radius of action, at her cruising speed of seven knots, of eighty-six nautical miles. (By courtesy of the RNLI)

A new No.2 motor lifeboat

With *William and Kate Johnston* installed as the No.1 lifeboat, a new motor lifeboat was built for the No.2 Station. The new boat, a 41ft by 11ft 8in Watson class, arrived at New Brighton on 20 December 1938. Powered by two 35hp Weyburn AE6 petrol engines, she had a top speed of 7.89 knots on trials, and a cruising speed of seven knots,

Edmond and Mary Robinson entering Princes Dock Liverpool, for her naming and dedication ceremony on 4 February 1939. On board are, left to right, William S. Jones, Coxswain John Nicholson, Harold Stonall, George Stonall, William Douglas, Edwin Smedley, William Liversage, Thomas Jones, Charles Flanagan and William Cross. (By courtesy of New Brighton RNLI)

The guests, station personnel and crew on board Edmond and Mary Robinson after her naming and dedication ceremony on 4 February 1939. (By courtesy of New Brighton RNLI)

at which rate she had a radius of action of eighty-six nautical miles. Built by Groves & Guttridge, of Cowes, at a cost of £6,534, she was provided out of a gift from Mrs Mary Robinson, of Liverpool, and was named Edmund and Mary Robinson. Her naming ceremony was held at the South West Princes Dock, Liverpool on 4 February 1939, when Mrs Robinson, then aged eighty-nine, christened the lifeboat. During the ceremony, the Lord Mayor of Liverpool, Sir Sydney Jones, presented the lifeboat crew with the medals awarded for the service to *Loch Ranza Castle* the previous month.

The scene in Princes Dock, Liverpool for the naming and dedication ceremony of Edmond and Mary Robinson on 4 February 1939. (By courtesy of New Brighton RNLI)

In exceptionally heavy seas and a severe north-westerly gale on the morning of 8 March 1939, the Crosby lightvessel broke adrift. *William and Kate Johnston* slipped her moorings at 11.55am and reached the lightvessel an hour and a quarter later. By that time, the lightvessel had pulled up to her emergency anchor, but was dangerously close to the shore near Formby. Coxswain John Nicholson, who had been in the post for just three months, took the lifeboat into the pounding surf and, after several attempts, got close enough to be able to rescue the crew of five. The lifeboat suffered considerable damage during this rescue, before all the men were safely aboard. They were landed at 3pm and the lifeboat was immediately placed off service so that repairs to her could be carried out. This particularly arduous service resulted in the RNLI granting additional monetary awards to each of the lifeboatmen involved.

Edmund and Mary Robinson answered her first service call on 11

Edmund and Mary Robinson was powered by twin 35hp Weyburn engines, but also carried auxiliary sails. (By courtesy of the RNLI)

June 1939. She slipped her moorings at 9.26pm in choppy seas and a stiff northerly breeze after the Police had reported that the motor boat *Sally*, of Birkenhead, was in difficulties off Seacombe Stage. The lifeboatmen found the casualty with three men, who had been out on a fishing trip. The boat's rudder and stern-post had been damaged and she was leaking badly. The three men were rescued and their boat was towed back to New Brighton at 10.30pm.

Wartime service

During the Second World War, both New Brighton lifeboats were kept very busy, and many services involved helping casualties of the conflict. The work of the lifeboat crews was often undertaken in extremely difficult and dangerous conditions, and the lifeboat crews had to deal with not only the natural hazards such as wind and tide, but the threat of enemy aircraft and bombing was constant. Aids to navigation, such as leading lights and lighthouses, were rarely shown, so the lifeboat crews found navigating to be much more difficult.

The first service undertaken in wartime came on 24 November 1939 and proved to be one in which the lifeboat saved more than 100 people. *William and Kate Johnston* put to sea at 10.25pm, in a fresh north-westerly wind, choppy seas and rain and hail after a vessel was reported to be aground on the revetment, inshore of the Beta Buoy. The lifeboat reached the scene within an hour and found the 8,000-ton cargo passenger liner *Pegu*, of Glasgow, with 103 people on board, listing heavily to port. Coxswain Nicholson immediately took the lifeboat alongside and rescued all the people, transferring them to pilot boats which were waiting nearby. The lifeboat then stood by *Pegu* until 7am, when she put twenty-three

Service Listing for 1940

Date	Lifeboat	Casualty	Outcome
Jan 4	William and Kate Johnston	HM Destroyer Whirlwind	The destroyer Whirlwind went ashore on the West Training Wall; she had a crew of 124, and over 100 were taken off by the lifeboat.
Jan 8	William and Kate Johnston	Norwegian steamer Maurita, of Bergen	Although stranded, the steamer Maurita did not need help as she was in no immediate danger.
Jan 17	William and Kate Johnston	A steamer	A steamer, reportedly mined, but could not be found and the naval authorities later reported that she had sunk without loss of life
July 23	Edmund and Mary Robinson	Auxiliary fishing smack Alice, of New Brighton	Stood by the smack Alice, which was ashore on Burbo Bank, until the vessel, with a crew of three, refloated at 12.45am; the lifeboat then escorted her into the channel and to a safe anchorage.
July 29	Edmund and Mary Robinson	Steamship Ousebridge, of West Hartlepool	Lifeboat put out at and found a pilot boat with thirty-seven survivors from the steamer Ousebridge, which had struck a mine. A pilot boat was towing the ship's boat, so the lifeboat took over the tow.
Oct 5	Edmund and Mary Robinson	Steamship Aquilla, of Liverpool	Lifeboat launched to the steamer Aquilla, which had a broken down engine in Formby Channel and was drifting in a moderate westerly gale. A tug was helping, and the lifeboat escorted them into dock.
Oct 13	Edmund and Mary Robinson	Blenheim aeroplane	A Blenheim aeroplane had been shot down in error by a British fighter, but a search, carried out during an air-raid, was without result.
Oct 21	Edmund and Mary Robinson	A British bomber	A bomber had come down in the sea, and the lifeboat found the tail of the aircraft above water but no sign of the crew of five.
Nov 2	William and Kate Johnston	Motor vessel Bolham, of Chester,	Lifeboat launched at 3.59pm in a south-westerly, but returned at 4.10pm having received a message that the crew of the casualty, Bolham, of Connah's Quay, had already been taken off by the vessel St Silio.
Nov 15	William and Kate Johnston	Steamship Penrhyn, of Liverpool	Lifeboat was found the steamer Penrhyn had been sunk in a collision. Her crew of five had been taken aboard the examination vessel Galatea, so the lifeboat brought them ashore.
Nov 21	William and Kate Johnston	Steamship Nord Est II, of Belfast	Lifeboat left her moorings at 8.55pm to help the steamer Nord Est II, a former French vessel, which, laden with petrol for Dublin, had gone aground. The crew stayed on board, despite the fore deck being awash, so the lifeboat stood by until at 2.10am when the steamer refloated.
Nov 23	Boarding boat	Men overboard from the steamship Biafra	The boarding boat, manned by two mechanics, put out at 2.30pm to the steamer Biafra, lying off New Brighton. As they reached Biafra, one of the steamer's boats was picking up a man in the water. Another man was in the river, so the two boats searched but without success.
Dec 6	Edmund and Mary Robinson	Steamship Governor, of Liverpool	Lifeboat found the steamer Governor out of control, with a tug trying to get a hawser on board. The lifeboat stood by, and then escorted them into the river. At 5.45pm the No.1 lifeboat put out with the coxswain, second coxswain and one lifeboatman from this service.
Dec 6	William and Kate Johnston	Steamship Gorsethorn, of Liverpool	The steamer Gorsethorn was disabled thirty miles from the station in a very heavy gale, so William and Kate Johnston put out. One sea swept over the lifeboat and nearly washed away two of her crew. She searched for a long time, not returning to station until 1.40am on 7 December.
Dec 7	William and Kate Johnston	Steamship Gorsethorn, of Liverpool	Gorsethorn was reported in need of immediate help fifteen miles north-west of the Bar Lightvessel; lifeboat launched, but immediately came news that Gorsethorn had been abandoned and her crew rescued by another steamer, and the lifeboat was recalled. In view of the severity of the first service, an increase was made in the monetary rewards.
Dec 8	Edmund and Mary Robinson	Formby Lightvessel	The Formby Lightship collided with an unknown vessel, so the lifeboat was launched and was asked by the master to stand by. As the weather was getting worse, the lifeboat eventually saved the lightvessel's crew.
Dec 23	Edmund and Mary Robinson	Motor vessel Ystroom	The Dutch motor vessel Ystroom, of Amsterdam, had been attacked and sunk by the enemy, but a later message said that the crew were safe.
Dec 27	William and Kate Johnston	Steamship Lady Connaught, of Dublin	The lifeboat put out to a vessel that had been mined ten miles north-west of the Bar Lightvessel. She found the vessel Greystone taking passengers from the steamer Lady Connaught, which had been mined. As there were too many for the lifeboat, Greystone took them to Liverpool.

men back on board to help tugs attempt to pull the vessel clear. But all the efforts failed and so the men were taken off again and the lifeboat returned to station at 11.40am. Two days later, *Pegu* broke in two.

During 1940 both New Brighton lifeboats were very busy, and the accompanying table lists all of the services, including those launches for which the lifeboat's services were not ultimately required. The first service of 1941 proved to be particularly hazardous, with the dangers coming not from the sea but from German bombs; the call had been received on 13 March 1941 at the height of a very heavy air raid in which Wallasey was badly hit, with *William and Kate Johnston* slipping her moorings at 9.15pm. She was the only boat then allowed to move on the river. All other craft had been stopped because of the danger from mines, which were known to be drifting upriver on the flood tide.

Fully aware of this additional hazard, and with bombs falling into the river, the lifeboatmen went to the aid of one of the victims of a mine, the 5,000-ton steamer *Ullapool*, of West Hartlepool. By the time the lifeboat reached the casualty she had sunk, with five of her crew being picked up by the steamship *Waldinge*. These men were taken aboard the lifeboat, which then searched upriver for the other members of the ship's crew but without success and the lifeboat returned to her moorings at midnight. Forty minutes later, the lifeboatmen were asked to go out again, to HMS *Virginia*, which had picked up nine of the crew of *Ullapool* and this they did, landing the men at 1.20am. Because of the additional dangers faced by the lifeboatmen during this service, the RNLI, granted additional monetary awards to each of them.

The New Brighton lifeboatmen were out in the early hours of 13 May 1941 after a vessel was reported to be in difficulties off the Egremont Landing Stage. *Edmund and Mary Robinson* slipped her

William and Kate Johnson during her early years on station at New Brighton, with the postcard boasting of her being the world's largest lifeboat. (From an old postcard supplied by John Harrop)

William and Kate Johnson at her moorings in the Mersey off New Brighton Pier. She was the only one of the four 60-61ft Barnetts with the exhaust coming out of the hull below the belting, just forward of the deck screen. In a beam wind the Coxswain and Mechanics could suffer from the fumes.

moorings at 1.45am and, in smooth seas and a light westerly breeze, made for the scene. However, the crew found that a large portion of the Landing Stage was missing, as the steamer *Westlands* had smashed into the Stage causing a large section to break away. This had on it a searchlight and a number of soldiers and it was drifting downriver. The lifeboat stood by this section until the Dock Board's vessel *Vigilant* arrived on scene, the lifeboat then going to *Westlands*. After the steamer had been pulled clear by tugs, the lifeboat returned to her moorings at 4.25am.

Early on the afternoon of 1 January 1944 a request was received to take a seriously ill soldier off one of the Coastal Defence Forts built in the Mersey Estuary, near the Burbo Bank. The Coastal Defence Forts consisted of a group of buildings, connected by

A fine photograph of William and Kate Johnson during her early days on station. (From an old postcard supplied by John Harrop)

bridges, on massive concrete piles; each Fort was about 70ft in length and had heavy anti-aircraft guns mounted on them. A very heavy sea was running, with a near gale force south-westerly wind and, as no other boat could attempt the rescue, *William and Kate Johnston* was called out. She slipped her moorings at 1.45pm and reached the Fort ninety minutes later. The sick man was lashed into a stretcher and lowered by ropes from one of the bridges, which, at times, were 40ft above the waves.

With the lifeboat rising and falling 15ft in the heavy seas, and with the soldiers not being used to handling ropes, it was extremely hazardous. But with great skill, Coxswain Nicholson held the lifeboat in position while the man was taken aboard. The lifeboat sustained some damage when she struck one of the concrete piles, but she got clear safely and the sick man was landed at Birkenhead at 6.30pm. Additional monetary awards were made to each of the lifeboatmen involved in what had been an extremely arduous service.

During the Second World War, lifeboats all round the coast were called out many times to aircraft which had ditched into the sea, and in the Dover Straits a specially-designed 64ft lifeboat was built specifically for this purpose. Occasionally survivors were rescued, but more often just wreckage was found, or patches of oil was all that was left of an aircraft. So when, on 13 December 1944, *Edmund and Mary Robinson* saved an aircraft, it was something of an unusual occurrence. The Coastguard reported that an aeroplane had come down into the Mersey off the Gladstone Dock, so the lifeboat put to sea just after 2pm in dense fog to search for the casualty. The lifeboatmen found a Walrus amphibious aeroplane, which had been forced to land in the river having run short of fuel. The lifeboat took the aeroplane in tow and returned to station at 5pm, placing the plane on moorings. During the next five days the lifeboatmen helped to refuel the plane and she was eventually able to take off again and return to base.

Just over two weeks after the aircraft service, *Edmund and Mary Robinson* was out again, this time in dense freezing fog on the afternoon of 28 December 1944. She went to the ferry *Wallasey*, which, loaded with passengers, had gone ashore just north of Seacombe. The lifeboat slipped her moorings at 5.20pm and Coxswain Nicholson had to carefully work his way along the river at very slow speed. The lifeboat reached the ferry at 6.30pm and immediately took off sixty-one women and children, landing them at Seacombe Ferry, before returning to *Wallasey* to take off another forty-one women, children and servicemen. After they had been landed, the lifeboat returned to Wallasey and the lifeboatmen found that she had refloated, so they stood by while the ferry slowly made her way to Seacombe Ferry, where the remaining 200 passengers were landed. Visibility was then virtually zero and so the lifeboat had to be moored at Seacombe where she remained until 5am the next day, by when the fog lifted sufficiently for her to be able to return to station.

The final services of the war were routine affairs. On 29 March 1945 *Edmund and Mary Robinson* was launched at 3.50pm to the fishing boat *Agnes*, which was ashore on the Burbo Bank in heavy seas. There was not enough water to get alongside so the lifeboat went back for a punt and the crew used it to take off the two men and the boy who were on board. On 9 June 1945 the motor boarding boat put out at 10.40pm to go help the naval cadet boat *Freelance*, which was dragging her anchors north of New Brighton pier and had a swamped engine room.

The boat was unable to tow the casualty, but rescued the nine officers and cadets on board. At 11.30pm, as the casualty was striking the piles of New Brighton pier, the No.1 lifeboat *William and Kate Johnston* was launched. The crew found *Freelance* partly under the pier and, at some risk went alongside, one lifeboat crew went on board and fastened a tow rope and the lifeboat then

towed *Freelance*. During the evening of 29 June *William and Kate Johnston* went to help the harbour defence launch 41360, which was ashore in the Crosby Channel. The water was too shallow for her to go alongside so she stood by until the rising tide refloated the launch, and then escorted her into New Brighton.

A routine event turned into a rather dramatic incident on 11 June 1946, when the RNLI's District Engineer and the District Hull Surveyor visited New Brighton to undertake a routine inspection. Motor Mechanic John Bray got into the boarding boat, which was held in davits at the rear of the Landing Stage, together with the two RNLI visitors, intending to go out to the moored lifeboats. But, without warning, one of the davit chains snapped and the three men were thrown into the water. At great personal risk, Motor Mechanic Bray rescued the other two men and was later awarded a Silver medal for Gallantry by the Liverpool Shipwreck and Humane Society.

On 22 September 1947 during, a violent south-westerly gale and heavy squalls, the Military Authorities became very concerned for the safety of Queen's Fort, one of the defence structures built in the Estuary and especially for the six men who were on the Fort. The Forts consisted of a group of towers each on four tubular piles leaning inwards, while the towers themselves projected beyond the piles. A motor launch from the Docks Board had already tried to take the men off the Fort, but with seas in the Mersey breaking up to 20ft high and the conditions appalling, had been unable to get

Edmund and Mary Robinson in the Mersey, passing the relief 45ft Watson motor City of Bradford, the No.1 lifeboat, at her moorings. (By courtesy of New Brighton RNLI)

close enough, so *William and Kate Johnston* was called out. She left her moorings at 2.45pm, under the command of Second Coxswain William Jones. He had held his post since 1938, but had never been in command of the lifeboat on service before.

Apart from the poor weather, Jones' task was made especially difficult by the construction of the Forts, as the piles offered no lee to the lifeboat, and as the towers projected out at the top getting close to them was extremely difficult. Once on scene, the Acting Coxswain had to hold the lifeboat in position by skilful use of the engines and rudder, as ropes were of no use. When he brought the lifeboat alongside one of the piles, one man jumped and was grabbed by the lifeboatmen and pulled aboard. Time and again, Acting Coxswain Jones had to take the pitching, rolling lifeboat close to the piles to rescue the men. The boat was in danger of being crushed beneath the massive superstructure as she was lifted high on each wave, while the next minute she was 20ft below the Fort. The lifeboatmen standing on the open foredeck were in extreme danger as they waited to grab hold of each man. But in the space of forty minutes all six men were rescued and nobody was injured, although the lifeboat received some minor damage.

This outstanding service had been completed in the most difficult of circumstance, demanding great courage from Acting Coxswain Jones, who handled the boat with great skill in a series of dangerous manoeuvres; for his superb seamanship Jones was awarded the Bronze medal by the RNLI; the Thanks Inscribed on Vellum was awarded to Motor Mechanic William MacDonald, who had operated the controls of both engines single-handed

Edmund and Mary Robinson at her moorings in the Mersey off New Brighton. (By courtesy of the RNLI)

Edmund and Mary Robinson taking on board an injured man from a cargo vessel.

throughout the service; and additional monetary awards were made to the other six members of the crew.

Early on the afternoon of 18 January 1948 the lifeboat was called out after the Formby coastguard had seen flares. As the lifeboat crew went out to the No.2 lifeboat *Edmund and Mary Robinson* in very rough seas in the boarding boat, one of the crew was washed overboard as the boarding boat went alongside the moored lifeboat. When he was hauled back on board by his colleagues, he was unconscious but fortunately he quickly recovered and was able to continue on service. The lifeboat slipped her moorings at 2.45pm and found the casualty to be the motor vessel *Guloy*, of Bergen. The master informed the lifeboatmen that he wanted a pilot, but, as it was too rough to put anyone on board, the lifeboat guided the vessel upriver to a safe anchorage.

The Mersey Estuary's wartime Defence Forts were demolished in 1947 and 1948, and the RASC Tender *Sir Herbert Miles* was used to transfer the workmen to and from the Forts during the work. On 28 January 1948, while engaged in this work, the tender ran aground on the revetment and so *Edmund and Mary Robinson* was called out to help at 5.42pm. The lifeboatmen found the tender had a serious list and so went alongside and rescued twenty-five men. The master then informed Coxswain Nicholson that another nine men were in a small boat on the other side of the revetment. Using the searchlight, the lifeboatmen spotted a small boat and

William and Kate Johnston at moorings on the Mersey, her home for more than twenty-seven years.

called to the men to row alongside the training wall.

Once they had done this, Coxswain Nicholson manoeuvred the lifeboat as close as he could on the other side of the wall so that ropes could be thrown across to the men who, one by one, were hauled through the water, across the top of the training wall and into the lifeboat. Two of the men injured their legs during this operation, but once everybody was safe the lifeboat returned to station at 7.30pm and landed the survivors.

What proved to be the last services by *William and Kate Johnston* were performed in 1949. At 6.20pm on 7 August she went to the converted ship's boat *Margie*, of Wallasey, with six on board and her engine broken down, dragging towards the Burbo Bank. The lifeboat rescued her crew, took their boat in tow and moored her off Egremont. At 3.10pm on 2 September 1949 she stood by the three-masted schooner *Susan Vittery*, which had gone aground, and escorted her to a safe anchorage when she refloated.

Three days later the lifeboat went to the fishing boat *Greyhound*, with three men and a boy on board; the boy had fallen on the engine, putting it out of action and badly injuring himself. The lifeboat wirelessed for an ambulance to be ready and towed the boat to New Brighton, where she landed the boy and took *Greyhound* to an anchorage. The final service came on 16 September 1949, when the yacht *Blue Waters*, with a crew of two, was towed into the Mersey. The seemingly routine service for the lifeboat crew became more challenging when, as they turned by the Crosby lightvessel, the owner of the yacht was washed overboard. The lifeboatmen immediately cut the tow rope and rescued the man from the water, after which a lifeboat crew boarded Blue Waters and the tow was completed without further incident.

In 1949 the RNLI announced that New Brighton was to receive a new lifeboat which would replace both No.1 and No.2 lifeboats. The new boat was completed in September 1950 so Coxswain Nicholson and some of the lifeboat crew travelled south to collect their new craft from the her builder, J.S.White, of Cowes. While they were away, another fine rescue took place off New Brighton, and one which proved to be the last by *Edmund and Mary Robinson*.

On the afternoon of 16 September 1950 the lifeboat was called out in a southerly gale and very rough seas with frequent heavy squalls after the Coastguard spotted a three-masted schooner at anchor in the Crosby Channel. After distress flares were seen being burned by her crew at 8.30pm, the lifeboat crew was immediately alerted and *Edmund and Mary Robinson* put to sea at 8.45pm, under the command of Second Coxswain William Jones. In truly dreadful conditions, with driving spray reducing visibility to almost zero, the crew had to use the searchlight to try and find the casualty and it was 9.30pm before they eventually found the vessel, the schooner *Happy Harry*, of Arklow, which had a crew of four and was lying alongside the revetment, a wall of limestone rubble 12ft wide which had been built on both sides of the channel to hold back the sand and prevent the main channel from silting up.

William and Kate Johnston approaching the New Brighton Landing Stage. (By courtesy of New Brighton RNLI)

The medal winning lifeboatmen of 1950 were presented with their awards at the RNLI's Annual General Meeting at Central Hall, Westminster, London on 13 March 1951, and included Second Coxswain William Jones (pictured centre left), who received the bar to his bronze medal, which he won in 1947. The other awardees were Coxswain Edward Kanavah (left), of Wicklow, who received the Bronze medal for a service to the motor vessel Cameo; Coxswain Patrick Power (centre right), of Dunmore East, who received a bar to the Bronze medal, for rescuing the crew of the fishing boat St Declan in a south-east gale, with squalls of snow, on 14 December 1950; and Second Coxswain Richard Power (right) , of Dunmore East, the Bronze medal for the same service.

Huge waves were sweeping over the vessel making it impossible to get alongside her from windward, and the waves were breaking heavily on top of the revetment. Acting Coxswain Jones knew that the top of the wall was very uneven and, in a number of places, there were slight gaps in it. With the schooner heeling right over the wall, he believed that if he could get onto the other side of the wall, he would probably be able to get under the lee of the schooner and rescue the crew. So, he began looking for a gap in the wall and, eventually, found one. By the light of the searchlight, he drove the lifeboat straight towards the gap and got across the wall safely. She bumped several times on the sandbank on the other side, and her last bump brought her bows against the schooner.

One of the lifeboatmen threw a line on board, but it was not needed. With the engines working ahead, Acting Coxswain Jones swung the lifeboat round and brought her bows up against the schooner and held her there, using the engines and rudder most skilfully. The four men who were on board the vessel quickly jumped aboard the lifeboat, which was backed away and then

Liverpool Shipwreck and Humane Society presentation at Liverpool Town Hall in 1950. From left to right: Jack Hatton (with glasses), bowman of Hilbre Island lifeboat; Coxswain Herbert Jones from Hoylake; New Brighton's Second Coxswain William S. Jones; and John William Bray, with the Mayor.

driven back over the revetment again and they arrived back at New Brighton at 11.15pm.

This remarkable rescue had demanded great skill, expert seamanship and a great deal of courage on the part of the Acting Coxswain, and was only possible because of the considerable knowledge that he and his crew had of the area. The RNLI awarded Acting Coxswain Jones a Bronze medal, his second, with additional monetary awards to each of the other crew members.

In September 1950 the new lifeboat arrived on station, and so both *William and Kate Johnston* and *Edmund and Mary Robinson* were withdrawn, and the station operated just one lifeboat from then on. Both had given outstanding service during their time on the Mersey: the Barnett was credited with saving 248 lives during her twenty-seven years of service, while the smaller Watson had launched sixty-nine times and saved eighty lives in just twelve years, with several outstanding medal-winning rescues undertaken.

After leaving New Brighton, *William and Kate Johnston* was sold out of service in December 1950, after being stripped of engines, batteries and specialist equipment. Her new owner renamed her *Jymphany* and fitted two 45hp Gleniffer paraffin motors in 1951. Then, he sailed the boat from the Mersey via the west coast, the Caledonian Canal and the east coast to the river Thames. A conversion was begun, but had hardly got under way before Turner got married and put the boat on the market as she was.

She was then sold to Lionel Law in early 1953. He took her to Salcombe, where she was converted at Winters Yard. The alterations included shifting the engines from amidships to the aft cabin, and the drive to the propeller shafts was by chain as the engines were positioned above the shafts. Cabin accommodation, providing eight berths, was built in the space forward of the new engine room. The air boxes were removed and doorways cut

William and Kate Johnston
decommissioning and
leaving New Brighton for
her last trip, 13 September
1950. Harold Stonall is
waving. (By courtesy of
New Brighton RNLI)

through the steel bulkheads to permit passage from one cabin to
another below decks. She was converted to a ketch rig by moving
the existing signalling mast aft and fitting a new mainmast, and
twin oil four-cylinder 58bhp Perkins L4(M) engines were fitted in
1956. Mr Law and his family cruised in her visiting many ports in
the West Country as well as going as far as Brittany.

In 1987 she was sold again and moved to Hartlepool, where she
remained there for much of the 1990s, but fell into a semi-derelict
condition. However, she was out of the water and was restored by
a new owner and renamed *Nexus*. She was fitted with twin Ford
Transit diesels, and brought back to seagoing condition. In 2000
Alexander Thomson bought the boat, have her back her original
name *William and Kate Johnston*, and moved her to Newsons Boat
Yard, Oulton Broad, for overhaul. She was used as a sailing boat out
of Ipswich Haven Marina, moving to Chatham in 2002.

She has travelled quite extensively, and returned to visit New
Brighton in June 2003, attending the Mersey River Festival. She
also attended the Fowey ex-lifeboat rally the same month. In June
2004, while off Anglesey, she was holed and had to be beached
at Rhoscolyn with the assistance of the Holyhead and Trearddur
Bay lifeboats. But she was repaired at Holyhead Boatyard and then
taken back south again. She was moved to Ramsgate in summer
2005 and was kept in the inner harbour for some time, used as
a training boat. She went to Ostend Harbour in 2009 and then
returned to Ramsgate. She attended the 70th anniversary of the
Dunkirk evacuation in May 2010, and alternates her moorings
between Ramsgate and Dover.

After her stint at New Brighton, *Edmund and Mary Robinson*
served in the Reserve Fleet for a further thirteen years, serving at
stations on the south coast and in Wales. Her most famous rescue

Above: William and Kate Johnston was converted into the motor ketch Jymphany in the 1950s and cruised around West Country ports under the ownership of Lionel and Sheila Law.

Left: William and Kate Johnston out of the water at Hartlepool in the late 1990s prior to being restored.

William and Kate Johnston on the Mersey in June 2002 during her historic return to New Brighton and Liverpool when she participated in the Mersey River Festival. (Nicholas Leach)

William and Kate Johnston moored at Ramsgate in March 2007 in the inner basin near Maritime Museum and several other historic vessels. (Nicholas Leach)

came in 1959, when she was on duty at Moelfre and she was used for the rescue of all eight crew from the stricken freighter *Hindlea* in hurricane-force winds, a service for which Moelfre Coxswain Richard Evans was awarded the Gold medal. She was sold out of service in March 1964 to a Mumbles-based owner, was renamed *Yoko* and was initially used as a rescue boat for Swansea Diving Club on the river Taw. She was later converted into a pleasure boat and named *Maid of Troy*, moving to the Worcestershire area during the 1990s, first to Tewkesbury and then to Worcester. She was rather neglected and ended up at Saul Junction on the Sharpness Canal. Following a change of owner in 2012, she was moved to Bromsgrove, where restoration work was started.

Edmund and Mary Robinson was converted into the pleasure boat Yoko and based at Worcester for many years. She was later renamed Maid of Troy, but her condition deteriorated and when she changed hands in 2014 she was in need to considerable refurbishment. (Courtesy of Grahame Farr)

Norman B. Corlett

O n 23 September 1950 a new lifeboat arrived at New Brighton, replacing both No.1 and No.2 lifeboats and leaving New Brighton with just one lifeboat, and becoming the sixteenth lifeboat at the station since 1863. The RNLI realised that it was no longer necessary for two lifeboats to be operated from New Brighton, and the new 52ft Barnett was more than capable of covering the area. The 52ft Barnett was the largest lifeboat type being built by the RNLI in the post-war era, and was the natural replacement for the 60ft Barnett *William and Kate Johnston* as well as *Edmund and Mary Robinson*.

A total of twenty 52ft Barnetts were built between 1950 and 1960, and the New Brighton boat, which was named *Norman B. Corlett*, was the first of the type. Fitted with twin 60hp Ferry diesel

The 52ft Barnett lifeboat Norman B. Corlett was built in 1950 by J.S. White at Cowes, Isle of Wight.

Norman B. Corlett on trials. She cost £29,264 and was provided out of a gift to the RNLI from W. Ernest Corlett and members of his family, in memory of his son, who had been drowned in a yachting accident. (Courtesy of New Brighton RNLI)

engines driving twin propellers, she had a top speed of just over nine knots and a cruising speed of eight knots, at which speed she had a radius of action of 188 nautical miles. She had a midship steering position, with cabins fore and aft.

The naming ceremony of the new lifeboat took place on 29 March 1951, at the South West Princes Dock, Liverpool and, despite steady drizzling rain, a large crowd turned out to greet HRH The Duchess of Kent, President of the RNLI. It was the first of two ceremonies attended by the Duchess at which she

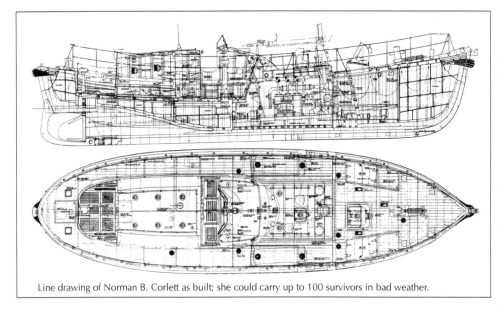

Line drawing of Norman B. Corlett as built; she could carry up to 100 survivors in bad weather.

performed the naming, with the other on 17 May 1951 at Margate. Shortly before noon the Duchess and her entourage arrived at the Dock, where the new lifeboat had been moored at an angle. The Lord Mayor of Liverpool, Alderman the Rev H.D. Longbottom, presided and welcomed the Duchess.

The lifeboat was formally presented to the RNLI by Mr W.E. Corlett, who said briefly, and with much emotion, 'On behalf of the Corlett family I have much pleasure in presenting this gift in memory of one who was very dear to us'. Commodore the Earl Howe, CBE, RNVR, Vice-Chairman of the RNLI, accepted the boat and handed her over to the New Brighton Branch. After the Earl of Derby had welcomed the lifeboat to Merseyside as chairman of the Port of Liverpool Branch, B.W. Harris accepted her on behalf of the New Brighton station. The Bishop of Liverpool, Dr Clifford Arthur Martin, assisted by the Rev W.L. Beckles Goodwin, Vicar of St James, New Brighton, and the Rev F.T. Copplestone, President of the Free Church Council, then dedicated the lifeboat, and the Duchess of Kent named her *Norman B. Corlett*.

By the time of her naming ceremony, *Norman B. Corlett* had already recorded her first service, on 10 February 1951, when she was called out at 10.14am in dense fog to look for a small boat with one man on board. The boat was eventually found, in the Rock Channel and was towed back to New Brighton. This was the first of 215 services she completed while based in the Mersey, and she saved 116 lives during her twenty-three-year career at the station,

The scene during the naming ceremony of Norman B. Corlett at the South West Princes Dock, Liverpool on 29 March 1951. (Courtesy of New Brighton RNLI)

Norman B. Corlett in the Mersey, where she was stationed for almost twenty-three years. (Courtesy of New Brighton RNLI)

The donor's plaque for Norman B. Corlett is displayed inside the current lifeboat house.

prior to entering the Relief Fleet. She was involved in several notable rescues, but many of her services were routine in nature, and the following descriptions are just a small number of the many incidents to which she was called.

At 2.55pm on 27 July 1951 the Wallasey Police telephoned a report that five people had been cut off by the tide on the North Bank. Two beach patrolmen were swimming out and the New Brighton Corporation rescue boat had put out, but had broken down, so at 3.07pm *Norman B. Corlett* left her moorings with a punt in tow and made for the North Bank. She found the rescue boat, and, leaving her at anchor, took aboard her crew of three, and one of the swimmers. While the lifeboat crew was searching, they received a radio message that more people were cut off near the Rock Lighthouse, but they got ashore by the time the lifeboat arrived. Another search was undertaken, but nothing was found so the lifeboat returned with the rescue boat in tow at 5.50pm.

Norman B. Corlett recorded her first life-saving service on 7 August 1951. She slipped her moorings at 1.47pm after the Coastguard had reported that a cutter-rigged yacht, the converted ship's lifeboat *Permit*, was in difficulties off Formby Point. The lifeboat found the casualty, with a crew of on board, and in rough seas and north-westerly gale, took Permit in tow to Rock Ferry. The lifeboat returned to her moorings at 6.40pm and the crew went ashore.

At 3.48pm on 14 June 1952 the Wallasey Corporation vessel Royal Iris wirelessed that she had seen smoke signals from a motor boat on the Burbo Bank, about two miles west-north-west of Burbo Buoy, and so Edmund and Mary Robinson, which was on temporary duty at the station, left her moorings under the command of Second Coxswain William Jones. A moderate sea was running, with a moderate westerly breeze. The lifeboat found a motor boat on board which were two men and four cadets from HMS Conway. Her engine had broken down. She was in heavy breaking seas and had been drifting for eight hours, so the lifeboat immediately took her in tow and brought her to Wallasey. The Commanding Officer of HMS Conway expressed his thanks to the lifeboat crew for their services.

At 12.20am on 15 August 1953 the coxswain was informed that a yacht was in distress off R.7 Buoy in the Rock Channel. So twenty-five minutes later Norman B. Corlett put out in a choppy sea, with a fresh south-west breeze blowing, and found the yacht Lesley, with a crew of four, a hundred yards north-west of R.8 Buoy. Her engine had broken down, and she was drifting over the Burbo Bank. The lifeboat rescued her crew and towed the yacht to New Brighton, reaching her station at 2.10am.

The boarding boats, which were kept hanging on davits at the Landing Stage, were used by the crews to reach the lifeboats moored in the river. (Grahame Farr, by courtesy of the RNLI)

On board Norman B. Corlett as she returned from service to the hopper barge James 96 on 24 August 1956. (Courtesy of RNLI)

At 10.03pm on 12 November 1955, a message was received from the port radar station that a coaster had been sunk in a collision near Formby light float. Seven minutes later *Norman B. Corlett* put out in smooth seas and a light north-easterly breeze. The lifeboat crew found that the steamship *Bannprince*, of Liverpool, had sunk after colliding with the steamship *Ocean Coast* near Beta buoy. Boats from *Ocean Coast* had rescued six of the coaster's crew, and another vessel had rescued the other three men and transferred them to a dredger. The lifeboat took the men from *Ocean Coast* on board and returned to station, where an ambulance was waiting, arriving at 12.50am on 13 November.

In May 1956 the reserve lifeboat *City of Glasgow*, a 51ft Barnett built in 1929, was placed on station temporarily while *Norman B. Corlett* was taken away for maintenance work. In the three months she was on station, the reserve lifeboat launched twice on service. *Norman B. Corlett* returned at the end of July and was called out on service on 1 August to the cabin cruiser *Merry Widow*. She was out on service again on the morning of 24 August 1956 after the Formby coastguard reported that a small vessel was in difficulties north of Formby float. *Norman B. Corlett* launched just after noon into rough seas and a moderate south-westerly gale. She found the hopper dredger *James 96* of London on Zebra Flats, but the crew of the dredger had sorted out the problem and the vessel was under way again. The lifeboat escorted *James 96* as far as New Brighton and then returned to station, arriving at 3.45pm.

John Rowlands Nicholson MBE, who retired at the end of December 1954 after serving as Coxswain for sixteen years. He was Second Coxswain for sixteen years, and had been awarded the MBE in 1951 for his work as Fishery Officer of the Lancashire and Western Sea Fisheries Committee. He was succeeded as Coxswain by George Stonall.

The first service of 1957 took place on the morning of 3 January when, at 9.35am, the marine surveyor of the Mersey Docks and Harbour Board telephoned to say that a member of the crew of the Bar lightvessel had been suddenly taken ill. As the Harbour Board's motor vessel *Salvor* was unable to get close to the lightvessel because of the rough seas, *Norman B. Corlett* put out at 10.07am

In 1954, the RNLI supplied a new boarding boat to the station, number BB-96. Built by Morris & Leavitt at Beaumaris, she measured 21ft 9in by 6ft 9in and was driven by a 15hp Enfield Mk.II diesel engine. The boat was provided from the proceeds of Panto Day, an annual fund-raising event organised by the students of Liverpool University. The gift of £4,000 was presented to the RNLI, and, in accordance with the wishes of the students, was used to fund the new boarding boat, which was named Panto. The photograph was taken on 20 February 1954 when the money was presented to the station and the University students went on board the lifeboat. The five lifeboat crew standing to the rear of the students are Second Coxswain W.S. Jones, Second Mechanic J. Christian, Coxswain J. Nicholson, Mechanic J.C. Bray and crew member W. Morris. (By courtesy of the RNLI)

to bring the sick man ashore. The lifeboat went alongside the vessel and the man was transferred across. The lifeboat then met *Salvor*, which had a doctor on board, , transferred him across and arrived back at her moorings at 2.15pm.

The last service of 1957 proved to be a particularly fine one. Shortly before 9am on 5 November 1957 the Coastguard reported that the 200-ton coaster *J.B. Kee*, of Castletown, was in difficulties, with a heavy list to port, in very heavy seas off Liverpool Bar. A southerly gale was blowing as *Norman B. Corlett* slipped her moorings at 9.20am, and she reached the coaster an hour later. She was lying beam-on to the wind and sea, listing forty-five degrees and her port rail was under water while her bridge deck was repeatedly disappearing beneath the waves as she rolled heavily.

Huge waves were sweeping clean over the small coaster and, from time to time, Coxswain George Stonall and his crew could see her starboard bilge keel coming out of the water, and this and the wide belting made it extremely hazardous for the lifeboat to approach the starboard side. Nevertheless Coxswain Stonall decided that her starboard bow offered the best chance of the lifeboat effecting a successful rescue. Using the loudhailer, Coxswain Stonall told the crew of the coaster to muster forward and he waited for the right moment before skilfully manoeuvring the port bow of the lifeboat alongside the starboard side of the coaster and called to her crew to jump. The lifeboat crew lined the deck and grabbed the coaster's six crew as they slid down into the boat. No one was injured and Coxswain Stonall brought the lifeboat away stern first, avoiding both the coaster's bilge keel and

Above: Survivors being landed from the coaster J.B. Kee on 5 November 1957. Philip Hockey has his back to camera on the landing stage.

Right: The lifeboat crew after the service to the coaster J.B. Kee, left to right: Charles Cooke, Harold Stonall, William Morris, William S. Jones, George Stonall, John Charles Bray and William Cross. (By courtesy of New Brighton RNLI)

her belting, as soon as the survivors were safe.

A tug later took the *J.B. Kee* in tow but, as she was being towed towards the port, the tow line parted and the vessel rolled over and sank. The lifeboat landed the survivors at New Brighton at 11.45am. For his excellent seamanship and great courage, Coxswain Stonall was awarded the RNLI's Bronze medal. The Institution's Thanks Inscribed on Vellum was awarded to Motor Mechanic Charles Bray, who had to operate the engine controls single handed as the Second Mechanic was away ill at the time.

At 10.40pm on 26 January 1959 the coastguard reported that the Dutch coaster *Toni* had reported seeing a distress signal from a boat near Rock Ferry. *Norman B. Corlett* launched at 11pm after this report had been confirmed into fresh south-easterly winds and choppy seas. The lifeboat crew reached the position and found a launch towing an ex-RNLI lifeboat, which was being used as a tender by a contractor working in the river at the new oil jetty. The crew of the ex-lifeboat had run short of fuel, so the lifeboat escorted the boats back to the contractor's ship and then returned to her moorings, arriving at 12.45am on 27 January.

Norman B. Corlett coming alongside the landing stage bringing in a small yacht. (Courtesy of New Brighton RNLI)

With the amount of shipping entering and leaving the Mersey, collisions between ships were not unknown, and on 18 July 1960 the lifeboat attended such an incident. The coaster *Denbigh Coast* and the steamship *Irish Maple* had hit each other when a mile east of the Formby light float, and *Denbigh Coast* was settling. *Norman B. Corlett* put out at 10.30pm and found that *Denbigh Coast's* crew of ten had already been rescued by other vessels by the time the lifeboat

Frank Neilson was appointed Second Mechanic in November 1957. Sadly, he lost his life in an accident in the Boarding Boat on 6 March 1962. During that afternoon he went out on his own in the Boarding Boat to the moored lifeboat but he apparently slipped as he tried to tie up alongside, fell overboard and drowned. He was succeeded as Second Mechanic by Arthur Maddock. (Courtesy of New Brighton RNLI)

Above and middle: Norman B. Corlett on service to the fishing boats Rosebud and Marion on 31 August 1958. She had launched at 12.30pm after a message had been received that a motor launch was in difficulties north of Seacombe stage. The lifeboat reached the position and found two boats, one a converted ship's boat and the other an old local fishing boat, secured alongside each other and lying to a single anchor. The anchor was not holding and, with the flood tide, the boats, which had nine people on board, were in danger of being swept under Seacombe landing stage. The coxswain manoeuvred the lifeboat alongside, and, after the second coxswain had cut the anchor rope, both vessels were taken in tow to Birkenhead. The lifeboat reached her station at 1.30pm.

Right: Norman B. Corlett at her usual moorings in the river. (By courtesy of New Brighton RNLI)

Norman B. Corlett at her moorings off New Brighton Landing Stage, on which can be seen the boarding boat suspended by davits. (Courtesy of RNLI)

The building used for the station's headquarters when the lifeboats were afloat in the Mersey was this house at 99 Egerton Street, pictured (left) in June 1970 and in use as a private house (above). (Grahame Farr, courtesy of RNLI; Nicholas Leach)

Mechanic Cyril Alcock (on left) and Second Mechanic John Kennedy outside the crew building at Egerton Street. (By courtesy of New Brighton RNLI)

arrived on scene. So the lifeboat towed in one of the ship's boats, and then returned to station at 3am on 19 July.

During the late 1950s and early 1960s the reserve lifeboat *White Star* was on duty several times at New Brighton. Built in 1930 for the Fishguard station in Wales, her first stint on the Mersey started on 29 November 1959 and lasted to 12 July 1960, with three services. She was again on station from 31 October 1961 to 30 April 1962, and again from June 1963 to November 1963, launching fourteen launches and saving nine lives during the latter stint, including a service on 22 June 1963 to a yacht in difficulty north of Rock lighthouse. Within ten minutes of the call coming, *White Star* had left her moorings with the bowman in command. There was a fresh north-westerly wind and moderate sea. The lifeboat crew found the yacht *Therese*, with two people on board, off the lighthouse. The yacht's engine had broken down, but her crew had managed to restart it, so the lifeboat escorted her up river as far as the lower buoy, reaching her station at 12.30pm.

Norman B. Corlett returned station in late 1963, but another reserve lifeboat, the 51ft Barnett *J.J.K.S.W.*, which had served at Stromness for more than twenty-five years, was on duty towards the end of 1964 ad undertook three services during her time on the

Norman B. Corlett returning from service, approaching the Landing Stage with a disbaled yacht in tow. (By courtesy of New Brighton RNLI)

Mersey, including one on 6 September 1964 to the cabin cruiser *Lucelle*, which had fuel trouble and had taken refuge alongside the Bar lightvessel in rough seas. She launched at 7am to help, by when the casualty was bumping against the side of the lightvessel.

En route, the lifeboat crew received a message that *Lucelle*, with a crew of four, had broken away from the lightvessel and a pilot cutter had intercepted her. Two of *Lucelle's* occupants were landed by the pilot boat, while the other two remained aboard to assist the lifeboat in towing their boat back to harbour. The lifeboat returned to station at 1.15pm.

Norman B. Corlett was back on station for 1965, and was called out on 24 August. At 6.35pm the coastguard reported that a dinghy in the Rock Channel needed help, and so at fifteen minutes later the lifeboat put to sea into a strong north-westerly gale and very rough seas The lifeboat found that the dinghy had beached off Harrison Drive and that her crew were safe, but the coastguard then asked if the lifeboat would search the sea and make sure that no other boats needed help. The Hoylake lifeboat *Oldham IV* had also been launched, to go to a yacht reported to be in distress in the river Dee, but the lifeboat was damaged during the launching operations off the beach, so the New Brighton lifeboat undertook the search. The yacht was later found to be at Mostyn so *Norman B. Corlett* returned to New Brighton, arriving back at station at 1.30am on 25 August.

New Brighton lifeboat crew returning from service. In the oilskins at the front are, left to right, G. Donnelly, George Cross, B. Morris, B. Cross and Cyril Alcock; at the back are, left to right, Tom Jones, Bev Brown, Bill Douglas, Dave Felton and D. Gilmoret. (By courtesy of New Brighton RNLI)

52ft Barnett Norman B. Corlett at moorings in the river. (From an old postcard supplied by John Harrop)

The year 1966 proved to be one of the busiest of *Norman B. Corlett's* time at New Brighton, with almost all of the services involving pleasure craft of some description, and most coming during June, July and August. On 1 June 1966 *Norman B. Corlett* went out in choppy seas to help a dinghy, which had capsized in the Rock Channel. The two survivors, who were found clinging to her, were taken on board the lifeboat, which took the dinghy in tow, and then went to the assistance of the West Cheshire sailing club's rescue boat, whose engine had broken down when attempting to help the dinghy. Two more dinghies were helped on 2 July 1966, with the lifeboatmen finding the two boats drifting in choppy seas after the engine of each boat had failed. A total of seven people were on board the two boats, and they were all rescued and their boats towed back to Garston Docks. On 9

New Brighton lifeboat crew in 1962. Standing, left to right: William S. Jones, Sydney Walker, William Cross, Arthur Maddock, John Bray, George Stonall (Coxswain) and John Kennedy; seated, left to right: Charles Cooke and Clifford Cooke. (Courtesy of RNLI)

August the lifeboat went to help a speedboat and a yacht, and 20 August assisted the cabin cruiser *Comet*.

The last service of the year was performed on 3 December, when *Norman B. Corlett* landed Captain Harold Hooton, master of the Bar Lightvessel, who had suffered a heart attack. In extremely bad weather, the lifeboat was taken alongside the vessel, with shelter being provided by three other ships, to take the master off together with Dr Thomas Shirkey. Dr Shirkey had gone out to help the casualty, and ended up staying on the lightvessel for five days. The master was brought ashore at the landing stage and taken to hospital by ambulance.

The services performed during the late 1960s were often routine in nature, usually involving the lifeboat towing in broken down vessels, such as that on 21 September 1969. At 7.59pm *Norman B.*

Miss Barbara Gorton being helped ashore from Norman B. Corlett after being rescued from the yacht Tricia on 5 August 1962. She was one of six people on board the yacht who were saved, with the yacht also being brought to safety. (Courtesy of RNLI)

Norman B. Corlett in the Mersey approaching the Landing Stage in January 1963. (By courtesy of RNLI)

Norman Dickinson (far left) and Fred Jamieson (with blanket) ashore after being rescued from a small fishing boat on 10 November 1963. They had been stranded at sea for five and a half hours, and Jamieson had tried to swim ashore. (By courtesy of the RNLI)

Corlett slipped her moorings in a gale force north-westerly wind with a rough sea to help a cabin cruiser in difficulties off New Brighton slipway. She found the cabin cruiser *Lara*, with two people on board, so towed her to moorings. A week later *Norman B. Corlett* brought in a dinghy with three people on board, and then a few days later left the station for a refit.

The reserve lifeboat *Crawford and Constance Conybeare*, built in 1939 and stationed at Falmouth for most of her time, came to New Brighton temporarily in 1969, and saved eight lives during a service on 18 October 1969. At 4.41pm a message was received that a boat was in difficulties half a mile west of the Rock light. At 4.55pm the reserve lifeboat slipped her moorings in a strong south-westerly wind and ten minutes later reached the two boats. The trimaran *Devil Woman* had run out of fuel and a cabin cruiser had experienced engine failure. Within half an hour, the lifeboat had taken both boats in tow and brought eight people to safety, returning to her moorings at 5.40pm.

At 3.20pm on 30 May 1970 the coastguard reported that the motor cruiser *Salazar* had broken down and was being carried over the Burbo bank, with two people on board. *Norman B. Corlett* slipped her moorings at 3.35 in a moderate westerly wind and a flooding tide. Although hampered by lack of water, the lifeboat and her crew succeeded in making a line secure to that they could take *Salazar* in tow. The tow was later transferred to the motor fishing vessel *Weaver*, and the lifeboat made for the yacht *Painted*

The lifeboat crew in the boarding boat, circa 1964. Standing, left to right: William Cross, Charles Cooke, John Kennedy, Sidney Walker, Inspector Harold Harvey, William Morris (Coxswain) and W.S. Jones (Second Coxswain); seated, left to right: 'Digger' Davies, David Felton, Cyril Alcock (Mechanic) and Victor Crossthwaite (RNLI fleet mechanic). (By courtesy of the RNLI)

The 1928-built reserve 51ft Barnett lifeboat J.J.K.S.W. towing the cabin cruiser Lucelle to safety into Wallasey Docks on 6 September 1964. A young Bev Brown, later helmsman on the Atlantic 21, on the left (at the bow) with John Williams; Coxswain Bill Morris is on wheel and his son Peter is far right. (By courtesy of New Brighton RNLI)

Norman B. Corlett at moorings in the Mersey, June 1966. The house in Egerton Street used as a crew facility can be seen above the lifeboat's bows. (Grahame Farr, by courtesy of the RNLI)

Above and left: Norman B. Corlett standing by during the Liverpool fire brigade give a demonstration of lowering a fireman from a Wessex helicopter onto one of the Liverpool tugs to deal with an imaginary fire on board, off the moorings at New Brighton on 15 June 1966. (By courtesy of RNLI)

The motor barge Middledale H, of Hull, on Canada Rocks near Langon Lock, 16 April 1967. Norman B. Corlett helped the vessel get off. (By courtesy of New Brighton RNLI)

Crew in Egerton Street about 1966 are Second Coxswain William (Billy) Cross, Coxswain William Morris and Mechanic Cyril Alcock. (By courtesy of New Brighton RNLI)

The reserve 51ft Barnett lifeboat Mary Stanford off New Brighton. She was on temporary duty at the station from December 1967 to February 1969. Built in 1930, she served at Ballycotton in Ireland until 1959, and was involved in the rescue from the Daunt Rock lightvessel, one of the most famous rescues in the history of the lifeboat service. (By courtesy of New Brighton RNLI)

Lady, which was aground on the bank. She stood by until the yacht refloated, and then returned to her station.

At 11.56am on 8 August 1970 *Norman B. Corlett* slipped her moorings, to go to the aid of a motor boat whose outboard engine had failed, leaving the boat drifting near the Burbo Bank in choppy seas and a fresh north-westerly wind. There were two men and two children on board the disabled boat and all four were rescued, with the lifeboat towing their boat back to New Brighton.

In choppy seas and a fresh north-easterly breeze, on the morning of 13 May 1972, a yacht got into difficulties off Wallasey and it was reported that her crew of two were in the water, so *Norman B. Corlett* put to sea just after 10am and rescued the two men. The yacht was anchored and the survivors were landed at 10.40am.

Norman B. Corlett was called out for what proved to be the last time on service at New Brighton on the afternoon of 24 January 1973. A cabin cruiser had capsized off New Brighton Pier and so the lifeboat slipped her moorings at 1.55pm. Together with the

Norman B. Corlett beached on the sands at New Brighton for a hull scrub in August 1967. In August 1963 she had a wheelhouse fitted over the previously open centre cockpit. In the autumn of 1968 she had a major overhaul, during which she was re-engined with twin 78hp Ford Thornycroft diesels. She was also fitted with radar.

Norman B. Corlett landing thirty passengers from the Mersey ferry Daffodil II on 8 September 1967. (By courtesy of RNLI)

Norman B. Corlett towing in a small boat that had broken down. Arthur Maddock snr is helming the casualty and his son, Arthur Maddock jnr, is the young crew member in line with lifeboat's mast, looking down the aft well. (By courtesy of the RNLI)

At the children's Christmas party in Egerton Street crew facility in 1963, crewman Bev Brown (on right) mentioned that Marie and he had just got engaged, and the local photographer took this photo of them.

boarding boat *Panto*, manned by two lifeboatmen, she made for the casualty. The two people from the cabin cruiser were found in the water and the boarding boat saved them, taking them to the Landing Stage. The cabin cruiser was taken in tow by the lifeboat and beached nearby, the lifeboat returning to her moorings at 3pm.

By early 1973 the RNLI had decided to change the status of the New Brighton station, and on 16 April 1973 *Norman B. Corlett* left the station having saved 116 ives in almost twenty-three years on the Mersey. She was taken to Anglesey Boatyard at Beaumaris, and entered the Relief Fleet. She spent eight years as a Relief lifeboat, during which time she saved a further twenty-one lives at various different stations. She was sold out of service in February 1982 and, renamed *Hannah*, was used as a workboat at Carrigaline, County Cork. She was sold on and converted to a ketch in 1998 with a deckhouse and accommodation below. She spent about a decade at Bangor Marina, Northern Ireland, having been given back her original name, and was offered for sale in 2010 as a houseboat.

During more than a century of service, between 1863 and 1973, the offshore lifeboats at New Brighton answered 676 service calls and saved a total of 1,040 lives. With the withdrawal of *Norman B. Corlett*, the station entered a new era.

Atlantic Lifeboats

With the gradual reduction in shipping using the Docks in and around Liverpool and Birkenhead during the 1960s and 1970s, the nature of the calls being answered by the New Brighton lifeboat changed. The great majority of services were to pleasure craft of various kinds, rather than the merchant ships that had been assisted hitherto. And change came to the station the lifeboat station as well, when, in 1972, it was announced that the New Brighton to Liverpool Ferry was to be withdrawn and the landing stage at New Brighton was to be demolished; this effectively made the continued operation of the station with a boat moored in the river impossible. The boarding boats used by the crew to reach the lifeboat's moorings were held on davits at the rear of the landing stage, and, as there was no other convenient place to keep them, they could no longer be used.

The first Atlantic 21 to serve at New Brighton was B-509, one of the early versions of the craft, pictured here without the roll bar which was later fitted above the twin outboard engines. (By courtesy of New Brighton RNLI)

As a result of the demolition of the landing stage, the RNLI decided to withdraw the all-weather lifeboat and replace it with a fast rigid-inflatable Atlantic type inshore lifeboat. Despite much

Mechanic John Richardson on the Fordson Major tractor, the station's first launch vehicle, approaching the launch site at Caithness Drive towing the Atlantic 21 B-500. (By courtesy of New Brighton RNLI)

The Fordson Major tractor pushes the Atlantic 21 B-500 across the beach to be launched, with D class inflatable D-42 already afloat. (By courtesy of New Brighton RNLI)

opposition from crew members, this was the only viable solution for the station. Once the decision had been taken, crew training on the new fast craft began and, on 16 April 1973, *Norman B. Corlett* was withdrawn, being taken to Anglesey boatyard at Beaumaris at which point she was placed in the Relief Fleet.

The Atlantic 21 class inshore lifeboats (ILB) that took over at New Brighton were then in their infancy, having been designed during the late 1960s by Rear Admiral Desmond Hoare at Atlantic College, at St Donat's Castle in South Wales. The first Atlantics were 21ft in length, and had a rigid hull on which was mounted an inflatable sponson. They were driven by twin 45hp outboard engines, which gave them a top speed of about thirty knots. The RNLI added a self-righting capability with an inflatable air-bag mounted on a roll bar above the engines at the stern, and the engines were inversion-proofed to enable them to restart after a capsize using a method devised by the RNLI. The three crew sat on a delta-shaped console in the centre of the lifeboat, the helmsman steering with one hand on the wheel while adjusting the throttles with the other.

New Brighton's first Atlantic, number B-509, was provided out of a gift from Mrs F.M. Walker and became operational on 19 May 1973. Until a boathouse had been built, this ILB, on her launching trolley, had to be kept in a garage a mile and a half from the launch site and so a small D class inflatable ILB, D-42, was also sent to the station, remaining for about eighteen months. The D class ILB recorded the first rescue by an ILB at New Brighton while she

Left: The Roadless Case type L tractor T35, which was built in 1940 and served at Lytham St Annes from 1969 to 1973, was brought to New Brighton as backup to the Ford tractor, which often got bogged down in the mud on the beach.

Below: The County tractor launching B-509 during the evaluation trials as station crew assessed the best ways to get the Atlantic 21 to sea. (By courtesy of New Brighton RNLI)

The County tractor launching B-509 down one of the slipways at high tide. The slipways were side on to the seas, and this photo gives a good idea of the difficulties this could cause in getting the boat afloat. (By courtesy of New Brighton RNLI)

Atlantic 21 B-509 is put through her paces in the Mersey, with Bev Brown at the helm. (By courtesy of Jeff Morris)

was at sea on engine trials on 29 July 1973, when her crew saw a woman and seven children cut off on the Rip-Rap Bank by the incoming tide. As the ILB was taken through very shallow gullies towards them, the two eldest boys began wading towards the shore. The ILB rescued the woman and the other five children, and then picked up the other two boys and landed everyone safely.

In the spring of 1974 a new boathouse, opposite the Baths, was completed and, at the beginning of June, the first of the RNLI's new County class launching tractors, later designated TW1 and specially adapted for launching the Atlantic 21 class ILB, was sent to the station. This was provided by Mrs Walker, who had also funded the new lifeboat. The first Atlantic went on to give excellent service to the station, and proved to be an ideal craft for service in and around the Mersey estuary.

At 11.45pm on 8 June 1974 former Second Coxswain W.S. Jones called at the home of Senior Helmsman Bev Brown, to tell him of his concern for the safety of the fishing boat E.B.H. The boat had been beached earlier on Mockbeggar Wharf so that her crew could clean the boat's bottom, but the wind had risen to force six whipping up very confused seas. The two lifeboatmen hurried down to the promenade to assess the situation and could see that the tide was coming in around the fishing boat, which was lying stern-on to the incoming sea, with two anchors out.

Already, spray was going clean over her wheelhouse and so Bev Brown telephoned Honorary Secretary Captain Billington agreed that the lifeboat be launched to stand by the fishing boat until she

Dedication of the ILB boathouse by the Rev Bob Evans of the Mersey Mission to Seamen, with the crew in attendance standing by D-42, the D class inflatable which spent a year and a half at the station. They are, right to left, Phillip Hockey, Paul Heenan (suited), George Stones, Alan Boult, Bev Brown, Arthur Cartwright, Peter Wilson, James Sewell, Stephen Ferie, Clifford Downing, Anthony Richardson (behind Rev Evans), Anthony Steen and Gavin Littler. (By courtesy of New Brighton RNLI)

Dedication by the Rev Bob Evans of the Marley ILB boathouse, which was built on King's Parade opposite New Brighton Baths. (By courtesy of New Brighton RNLI)

was clear of the beach, and so the maroons were fired. The Atlantic 21 was towed by the tractor to be launched just north of the Pier. However, as the port outboard engine would not start and a very heavy surf was running in onto the beach at that site, it was decided to go to another launch site, at Caithness Drive, about a mile upriver, where it was more sheltered. The plugs on the outboard engine were cleaned and, at 12.20am, B-509 was launched with both engines working.

As the ILB rounded Perch Rock lighthouse she ran into very heavy breaking seas, made worse by the backwash off the seawall. Helmsman Brown found the fishing boat about 300 yards offshore and 150 yards west of a steel groyne being pounded by the heavy seas and rolling about thirty degrees either way. So the lifeboatmen dropped anchor and the ILB was veered down towards the fishing boat, but *E.B.H.* was being driven closer and closer to the seawall despite then having four anchors out.

Bev Brown's memories of the 1970s

Edward 'Bev' Brown started out as crew on the 52ft Barnett Norman B. Corlett, and was heavily involved in the early days of the Atlantic ILBs when the all-weather lifeboat was withdrawn, going on to become a double medal-winning helmsman.

'When the status of the station was changed in the early 1970s, it was not just a case of a conventional Lifeboat going and an Atlantic being put in its place. New Brighton, at the mouth of the Mersey, has a tidal range of over 30ft and a tidal ebb and flow of over seven knots. From the promenade, where all of the slipways are broadside on to the sea at high tide, to a quarter of a mile of beach, at the water, with quicksands and mud, launching areas were challenging to say the least. Most of the crew of Norman B. Corlett were too old to crew the Atlantic, and so a new crew had to be found, which was not easy. The old crew were also unhappy that the RNLI had closed the station, as they saw it, while those local people whose relations were or had been on the crew were also not in favour of what had happened.

On the practical side, Lieutenant Peter Rowe, the RNLI Inspector, was sent to get the Atlantic station up and running and he had a very difficult job. The box trailer used for launching, as the drive-off the trailer had not been developed, was a very basic affair. It had a small wheels which bogged down in the sand and the boat had to be launched stern first. B-500 was the first Atlantic at New Brighton. On one occasion about

Night-time launch of Atlantic 21 B-509 at high tide down one of the slipways into the river.

8ft of the sponson was ripped when we were trying to recover the boat. The tractor was an old Fordson Major type bought from Mold in North Wales at a farm auction by Peter Rowe and travelling mechanic G. Roberts. This got bogged down in the soft sand on many occasions, and an old Case tractor from Lytham St Annes was sent as a backup. Eventually, the RNLI successfully, trialled a four-wheel-drive Ford 7000 tractor which proved to be up to the job.

The boathouse at Egerton Street was used to house the clothing and equipment, but the Fordson Major tractor, which had large additional rear wheels to try to stop getting bogged down, was kept near what was left of the pier because there was no room for it and the boat and trailer in the large shed by Wallasey Grove Road railway station. When the boat was wanted, the crew went to Egerton Street for their gear and then, using their cars, drove to Grove Road station to get the boat ready. The mechanic would go to the pier and get the tractor and drive the mile and a half to the boat, hitch it up to the tractor, and then drive the same distance back to New Brighton to launch. It was like this until the boathouse was built on the site opposite the swimming baths still used today.

As this was clearly an unsatisfactory arrangement, the committee and crew were asked if they wanted to wait for a permanent boathouse to be built, which would take six months, or whether they would prefer Marley garage which could be erected in about two weeks. The decision was unanimous that the Marley garage was needed. In order to ensure that a boat was available to cover any close calls, D class inflatable D-42 was sent to the station and kept at New Brighton baths with the tractor, out of season, and then at Wallasey Yacht Club until the new boathouse was up and running satisfactorily.

When launching the Atlantic with the Fordson Major tractor, even with a small sea running, the tractor driver was usually soaked up to his waist in water. It was not much better when of the new tractor arrived as a running sea soon soaked the driver, and there were no

Helmsman Bev Brown on board Atlantic 21 B-509 with crew members Anthony Clare and Rodney Kluzeman. (By courtesy of the RNLI)

dry suits in those days. Launching when the sea was up to the promenade wall, because all the slipways were side-on to the sea, as the tractor backed the trailer down the slipway to launch, the waves could knock it sideways and out of alignment with the carriage. The tractor driver would therefore have to realign the rig and start the launch procedure all over again.

Determining the best place to launch was difficult, and knowing the beach was essential. Myself and tractor driver Brian Aves walked the beach on both sides of the old pier site one day, and went round to the Perch Rock Lighthouse, as far as Harrison Drive, covering about two miles while assessing possible launch sites and discovering areas of very soft sand and mud on low spring tides.

Once the lifeboat had launched, there was no contact between the boat and beach crew as the tractor was not equipped with a radio. When the boat returned, the shore crew would shout to those on the boat to agree on the best place to recover. The boat was not called 'New Brighton lifeboat', but used the call sign 'New Brighton Rescue' initially, and this was a bit of a downer for a lifeboat station with over a century of service. Looking back at the early days of the Atlantics, there were many problems, notably with the outboard engines, but the RNLI eventually got them waterproofed and the difficulties were overcome.

For the crew, there were no visits to headquarters to learn about the boat, the engines, or boat handling techniques, and we were basically thrown in at the deep end when it came to discovering the capabilities of the craft and its equipment.

But despite these rather difficult beginnings and the problems of the early days of Atlantic lifeboat operation, the different Atlantics have proved themselves time and again. The station went on to become extremely successful and the crew can be proud of their efforts and continuing dedication. 9

Atlantic 21 B-509 in the Mersey, with Dev Brown at the helm and crewed by Frank Brereton, Steve Ferrie and Gavin Littler. B-509 was on station from May 1973 to 1981. (By courtesy of New Brighton RNLI)

Atlantic 21 B-509 being taken down Caithness Drive to be launched, using tractor TW1. (By courtesy of New Brighton RNLI)

With their anchor rope fully paid out, the lifeboatmen were still twenty yards short of the casualty and so the ILB had to be re-anchored and Helmsman Brown again attempted to veer down. As the fishing boat's anchors dragged even further, the boat got still closer to the Promenade and further away from the lifeboat. As the lifeboatmen worked to attach their drogue line to the anchor-rope, the fishing boat struck the groyne and heeled right over to starboard, just ten yards from the seawall and in imminent danger of breaking up.

As heavy seas continued to pound the fishing boat, Helmsman Brown ordered the lifeboat's anchor rope to be cut and then, with great skill and tremendous courage, drove the ILB round the bows of the fishing boat and brought her up to the port side of the fishing boat, driving the ILB right onto her deck. Two of the fishermen were grabbed by the lifeboatmen and dragged aboard the ILB but the third man had injured his leg and was clinging to the rigging, up to his waist in water. Lifeboat crew Robin Middleton immediately volunteered to go aboard the fishing boat to get the man. The deck of *E.B.H.* was cluttered with lose gear and ropes and, as heavy seas swept over both boats, Middleton had great difficulty in reaching the fisherman, who was suffering from

The County tractor launching Atlantic 21 B-509 from the slipway facnig the Perch Fort. (By courtesy of New Brighton RNLI)

shock and exposure. The fishing boat was grinding on the steel groyne, as lifeboat crew Middleton carefully helped the injured man across the deck and into the lifeboat.

It was 1am and the three fishermen had been taken off, but returning to station was not straightforward. As Helmsman Brown backed the ILB clear and turned her round to head back out into deeper water, a rope from the fishing boat fouled the lifeboat's port propeller. So, with the starboard engine at full power to hold the boat head-to-sea, the port engine was stopped, raised and the propeller cleared. Then, on two engines again, the ILB got clear and headed back to the recovery site, where an ambulance was waiting to take the fishermen to hospital. It had been a truly outstanding

New Brighton lifeboat crew and station personnel in the late 1970s. (By courtesy of New Brighton RNLI)

The County tractor pushing the drive-on drive-off carriage into the water prior to recovery of the Atlantic 21. (By courtesy of New Brighton RNLI)

rescue and the RNLI awarded Silver medals to Senior Helmsman Bev Brown and lifeboat crew Robin Middleton, with the Thanks Inscribed on Vellum accorded to the other three members crew, lifeboatmen Clifford Downing, Alan Boult and Ian Campbell.

The Atlantic continued undertake rescue work, being very busy during July 1974 helping dinghies, yachts and speedboats. The following year, she was busy during the spring helping a couple of yachts on 7 May and bringing four people to safety after they had been cut off by the tide on 25 May. Three days later, after the Coastguard had reported that a boy was drifting out to sea in a rubber-dinghy, off Formby Point, the relief Atlantic 21 B-500 was launched at 2.35pm on what proved to be a straightforward service. In calm seas, but with a fresh north-easterly breeze, thirteen-year-old Stuart Nixon, of Liverpool, was rescued and landed nearby, into the care of the Coastguard. While on the face of it a routine rescue, this was a significant milestone as it was the 100,000th life to have been saved by the RNLI. To commemorate the event, a Certificate was later presented to Stuart and another to the New Brighton station.

Right: HRH The Duke of Kent presents Edward 'Bev' Brown with the Silver medal for gallantry at the RNLI's Annual Presentation of Awards in London in 1975. (By courtesy of New Brighton RNLI)

Below: Silver medal winners Robin Middleton (on left) and Bev Brown, who were involved in the service to the motor fishing vessel E.B.H. on 9 June 1974.

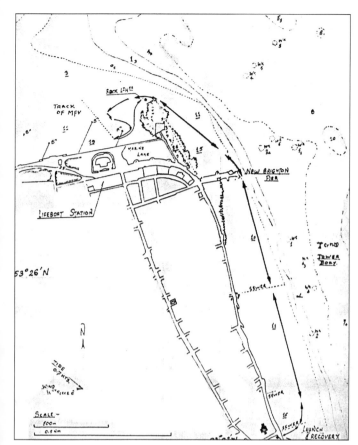

The track taken by the
Atlantic 21 to reach the
fishing vessel E.B.H. for
the medal-winning service
of 9 June 1974.

B-509 served at New Brighton from 1973 to 1981 and, having
already been involved in an outstanding-medal winning rescue, in
1976 she was used in what turned out to be another fine rescue.
She was launched at 5.40pm on 23 October 1976, after a yacht
had been reported to be, apparently, in distress. At the time, the
conditions were very close to the operating limits for the ILB,
with very rough seas and a south-westerly gale blowing but, under
the command of experienced Helmsman Bev Brown, the ILB
got away safely. The casualty, very close to the Training Wall, was
spotted by the lifeboatmen at 5.55pm. But, she was on the opposite
side of the Wall and so Helmsman Brown had to come back and
then go round the southern end of the Wall to reach her.

In worsening conditions, with the wind gusting to force nine,
he radioed for a helicopter and also asked for the Hoylake lifeboat
Mary Gabriel to be put on stand-by as the Atlantic having had
hit the bottom several times as she faced heavy surf and shallow
water with waves up to 8ft high, making progress was very slow.
Although the helicopter was on its way, along with a pilot boat
and the Hoylake lifeboat, conditions were getting even worse and
Helmsman Brown had difficulty in keeping the Atlantic 21 head

The first ILB house at New Brighton was built in 1973 and housed the Atlantic 21. It was used until 1989 and then demolished. (Jeff Morris)

Atlantic 21 B-509 on her launching carriage inside the first ILB house at New Brighton, which was used from 1973 until 1989. (By courtesy of New Brighton RNLI)

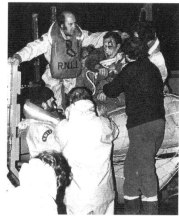

Three photographs taken in the early hours of 2 July 1977 showing the lifeboat crew undertaking a net recovery of Atlantic 21 B-509 to land an injured seaman from the Norwegian tanker Essi Karti. B-509 launched at Portland slipway at 4.50am. Honorary Secretary Captain John Billington tried to contact station medical advisor Dr J. Drury, but he was not available so an extra first aider was taken. Coast Guard informed that lifeboat crew that the casual tea was south of Liverpool Landing stage. When that Lifeboat was halfway to the casual tea the Coast Guard were asked to request an ambulance to be at Caithness Drive slipway and to ask the Lifeboat tractor and carriage and beach crew to also make their way to this site.

Injured crewman Arne Myhaus born in 1934 had face and head injuries after falling down the companionway but was conscious, so it was decided to taking off and land him for sure. At lifejacket and safety harness were placed on him and he was helped down a rope ladder by lifeboat crew R. Robertson and C. Downing. Another crewmen from the ship was also brought ashore. Lifeboat crew Frank Brereton acted as interpreter throughout the evacuation. Due to the backwash from the promenade wall, that recovery net was requested to be rigged and the seamen were landed at 1.30am and passed to the awaiting ambulance. The lifeboat returned to station minutes later to be washed down, refuelled and made ready for service.

A crowd watches as Atlantic 21 B-509 returns from service on 6 June 1976 to a broken down speedboat. (By courtesy of New Brighton RNLI)

Atlantic 21 B-509 returning from service on 6 June 1976, being hauled up the slipway. (By courtesy of New Brighton RNLI)

Shore crew wait on the carriage while Atlantic 21 B-509 is readied for recovery, using tractor TW1. (By courtesy of New Brighton RNLI)

Crew members being presented with Vellum Certificates, for the service to Annaliva, at Wallasey Yacht Club on 28 July 1977. The three crew are (from second left), left to right, Robert Robertson, Bev Brown and Christopher Pringle. (By courtesy of New Brighton RNLI)

to sea, battling waves up to 10ft high. The Coastguard then relayed a message from the crew of the pilot boat that the yacht had run aground and her crew were in the water.

As the ILB continued to make slow progress towards the scene, the helicopter flew over and, at 9.10pm, the lifeboatmen were informed by radio that the helicopter had rescued the crew of the vessel, *Annalivia*, an ex-lifeboat, so Helmsman Brown slowly turned the Atlantic round and headed back towards New Brighton, arriving there at 9.40pm.

For his outstanding seamanship and great courage during this incident, the RNLI awarded its Thanks on Vellum to Senior Helmsman Bev Brown, with Vellum Service Certificates later being presented to lifeboatmen Robert Robertson and Joseph Pringle. It had taken a great deal of skill and courage by the crew of the helicopter to rescue the crew of the yacht and the Winchman, Flight Sergeant John Donnelly was awarded a Bar to his Air Force Medal,

Lifeboat crew rush to prepare the Atlantic 21 after a call out was received during a station open day in the early 1980s. (By courtesy of New Brighton RNLI)

County tractor TW1 launching Atlantic 21 B-509 at high water. On station from 1974 to 1987, TW1 was the first of a new kind of tractor developed to launch Atlantic ILBs, and was based on a standard tractor that was marinised to enable it to be taken into water. Launching conditions at New Brighton are among the most challenging of any RNLI lifeboat station. (By courtesy of New Brighton RNLI)

with the Pilot, Flight Lieutenant Garnon Williams receiving the Queen's Commendation for Valuable Service In The Air.

B-549 Blenwatch

In the spring of 1981 a new Atlantic 21, B-549, was sent to New Brighton, and was funded by the Fred. Olsen Shipping Company, which has been a generous supporter of the RNLI for many years. At a ceremony on Sunday 19 July 1981, with a large crowd braving the rain, the new lifeboat was formally named *Blenwatch* after two of the company's cruise ships, *Blenheim* and *Black Watch*. The service of dedication was conducted by the Rev H. Baguley, vicar of St James and chaplain of the lifeboat station, assisted by the Rev P. O'Brien, parish priest of St Peter and Paul, and the Rev K. Nicholson, minister of St Andrews. Singing was led by the choir of St James and music was provided by Merseyside Police Band. At the end of the ceremony, Mrs Patricia Davies formally named the lifeboat, which was then launched for a short demonstration.

B-549 *Blenwatch* spent fifteen years at New Brighton and gave outstanding service, undertaking a number of fine rescues. One of these took place on 11 July 1981, when she was launched at 2.45pm, with Helmsman Ian Campbell in command, manned by lifeboatmen Anthony Jones, Mike Jones and Robert Robertson, in rough seas and a strong north-westerly force five wind to help the motor boat *Mary*, which was reported to be in difficulty off New Brighton bathing pool. The lifeboat first made for the position she

had been given off the bathing pool, where a number of pleasure boats were moored. Seeing one boat with a fishing party on board which appeared to be lying low by the stern, Helmsman Campbell went alongside, but it was not this vessel which needed help.

At this point, Helmsman Campbell decided that *Mary* must be further out to sea and further to the west, so he set off in that direction at full speed. While on the way, he received information from the coastguard that *Mary*, a 30ft former ship's lifeboat, was lying between Askew Spit and Little Burbo Bank, six miles north-west, and was being pounded by heavy surf with two people on board. The Atlantic 21 found *Mary* at 3.22pm and the owner's wife was taken on board while an attempt was made to tow the casualty into calmer water. Little headway could be made, however, as the boat was still taking water and her pumps could not clear it.

Helmsman Campbell decided that *Mary* should drop anchor and the owner be taken off. On the way back to station a request was made for an ambulance. After landing the two people at

Left: Atlantic 21 Blenwatch (B-549) about to launch after her naming ceremony on 19 July 1981. (By courtesy of New Brighton RNLI)

Below: Mrs Patricia Davies who named the Blenwatch (B-549). (By courtesy of New Brighton RNLI)

Atlantic 21 Blenwatch (B-549) being towed across the beach and launched for a short demonstration at the end of her naming ceremony, 19 July 1981. (Jeff Morris)

4.05pm, the lifeboat crew returned to *Mary* with the idea of taking her in tow again, but she had taken in much more water and it was decided to leave her and return to station. The Atlantic 21 was back at the slip at 5.05pm and was washed down, refuelled and ready for service at 5.45pm. By now *Mary*, which had been on passage from the Isle of Man to Birkenhead, was under water with only her mast visible and she was later found to have broken in two. For this service, a letter signed by Cdr Bruce Cairns, the RNLI's chief of operations, expressing appreciation to Helmsman Ian Campbell and his crew, was sent to the Honorary Secretary, Captain J.A. Billington.

A few months later, another challenging rescue was performed by the New Brighton volunteers. Just after 5pm on 13 September 1981 a yacht was reported to have grounded on the training bank off Buoy C6. Helmsman Bev Brown telephoned the honorary secretary of and, as preparations were being made to fire the maroons, a request came from Liverpool Coastguard to launch to the aid of the 28ft steel-hulled yacht *Blue Tango*. At 5.12pm B-549 *Blenwatch* was launched, manned by Helmsman Brown and crew members Anthony Clare and Robert Robertson. It was a fine, clear evening but with a fresh to strong breeze, force five to six, blowing from the south-west and gusting to near gale, force seven. The sea was moderate to rough and there was a moderate west-south-westerly swell.

Blue Tango was hard aground on the west training bank, seven miles north-west of the lifeboat station. On arrival, the Atlantic 21 ran the yacht's kedge anchor out into deeper water to the west to prevent her drifting further ashore as the tide rose, and shipping was asked to ease speed in passing. At 7pm, after a good deal of bumping and surfing in the heavy sea and swell in the making tide, the yacht floated free. The anchor held at first but then started to drag, and the yacht knocked across the training bank to the east.

The Atlantic 21 went round the end of the bank to meet her and escort her into the channel. In view of the deteriorating weather, however, and the yacht's slow progress, the lifeboat towed

Atlantic 21 Blenwatch (B-549) is recovered on 19 July 1981. (Jeff Morris)

After recovery, Blenwatch (B-549) is brought back across the beach on 19 July 1981. (Jeff Morris)

After recovery, Blenwatch (B-549) is brought back across the beach on 19 July 1981. (Jeff Morris)

After recovery, Blenwatch (B-549) is brought back to station, watched by supporters and well-wishers, on 19 July 1981. (Jeff Morris)

Lifeboat crew and station personnel with civic dignitaries outside the lifeboat station. Back row, left to right, Robert Barrass, Geoff Prince, Paul Edwards, Howell Williams, Barry Downing, George Stewart, Peter Shillinglaw and Tony Clare; front, left to right, Anthony Billington, Graham Lowe, Lady Mayoress, Cliff Downing, Steve Jones, the Mayor, Brian Aves and Eric Lowe. (By courtesy of New Brighton RNLI)

her to Alfred Basin. The lifeboat returned to station at 9pm and was rehoused and once again ready for service half an hour later. For this fine service a letter signed by Cdr Bruce Cairns, RNLI chief of operations, was sent to honorary secretary Captain J.A. Billington expressing the Institution's appreciation to Helmsman Bev Brown and crew members Anthony Clare and Robert Robertson.

On 29 August 1982 the New Brighton lifeboatmen undertook yet another outstanding rescue. *Blenwatch* was launched at 2.10pm after the Coastguard had reported that the yacht *Ocea* was acting in an erratic manner and appeared to be in difficulties, just north of the Great Burbo Bank. The ILB was manned by Senior Helmsman Bev Brown and lifeboatmen Mike Jones, Dale Kaye and Tom Baker. At the time, the sea was choppy, with waves up to 4ft high and a strong south-westerly wind. Another yacht, *White Out*, was standing by in the main-channel and she reported that, although they had asked the crew of *Ocea* to return to the Mersey, the yacht was continuing towards Hilbre Island.

Lifeboat crew outside the boathouse. Pictured, left to right, are Cliff Downing, Peter Adams, Robert Jones, Alister Gow, Dale Kaye, Geoffery Prince, Rod Kluzemann, Stephen Ferrie, Rear Admiral Arthur Heslett, Robert Barrass, Chris Pringle, Brian Aves, Robert Robertson, Salford supporter George, and Tom Baker. (By courtesy of New Brighton RNLI)

Lifeboat crew amd station personnel in the early 1980s. (By courtesy of New Brighton RNLI)

Lifeboat crew on board Atlantic 21 Blenwatch (B-549) are, left to right, Paul Edwards, Dale Kaye, Anthony Kaye, Anthony Clare and Anthony Jones, with Honorary Secretary Captain Tony Billington standing by the bow. (By courtesy of New Brighton RNLI)

As soon as the lifeboat reached the scene, *White Out* headed back to the Mersey, conditions by then having worsened with the wind force six, gusting to gale force, and waves 10ft high in the main channel. *Ocea* was on the other side of the revetment and was heading for Taylor's Bank, where the waves were building to 15ft in height. Helmsman Brown knew that the yacht was heading for trouble and so made straight for her. The ILB was violently thrown about in the heavy seas, and lifeboat crew Mike Jones injured his hip when he fell onto the port lifting eye. But before the ILB could reach *Ocea*, the yacht broached to and her crew appeared to lose control.

The ILB got to the yacht at 2.45pm and found two men on board, a father and his son, with the father totally exhausted. In view of the

Tractor TW1 and Atlantic 21 Blenwatch (B-549) outside the boathouse. (By courtesy of New Brighton RNLI)

Atlantic 21 Blenwatch (B-549) on exercise in the Mersey on 19 July 1981. She was one of only two Atlantic 21s that had windscreens mounted on the helmsman's console. (Jeff Morris)

prevailing conditions, Helmsman Brown decided that it would be too risky to try and take the men off the yacht and so, after two attempts, lifeboat crew Mike Jones was put aboard the yacht. He found that the bottom half of her rudder was missing, so it was decided to try and take the yacht in tow. Lifejackets were passed across for the two men and then, with the yacht in tow, Helmsman Brown set off northwards, having decided that it would be too dangerous to attempt to tow the yacht across Taylor's Bank. A bucket was streamed astern of the yacht, to act as a makeshift sea anchor.

At 3.55pm the Hoylake lifeboat *Mary Gabriel* was launched and, as she made her way at full speed towards the New Brighton

lifeboat and her tow, *Blenwatch* headed slowly northwards, towards Southport, at about three knots. When they were about two miles off Birkdale, a very heavy sea struck *Ocea* and knocked her over onto her beam ends and the emergency anchor was lost. The Coastguard then reported that conditions at Southport were too bad for the yacht to be beached there and so Helmsman Brown continued towards the Ribble Estuary. But, knowing conditions there would be too bad for the ILB to tow the yacht over the Bar at the entrance to the Estuary, he requested the Lytham St Annes lifeboat *City of Bradford III* be called out to help.

In waves up to 20ft high, New Brighton lifeboat rendezvoused with the Lytham St Annes lifeboat at 5.30pm and the tow was transferred. It was decided to put the two yachtsmen on board the Lytham boat and, after several attempts, the two men and Mike Jones were taken aboard the Atlantic 21 and the yachtsmen were transferred to the Lytham St Annes boat which, at 6pm, began towing Ocea over the Bar and into the Estuary. *Blenwatch* then turned round and began heading back, meeting the Hoylake lifeboat at 6.15pm and they returned together, with the ILB being beached at New Brighton at 8pm.

For this truly outstanding service, Senior Helmsman Bev Brown was awarded the Bronze medal by the RNLI. The RNLI's Thanks Inscribed on Vellum was awarded to lifeboat crew Mike Jones, with Medal Service Certificates being presented to lifeboatmen Dale Kaye and Tom Baker.

Lifeboat crew outside the boathouse in the early 1980s. Back row, left to right, Dale Kaye, Mike Haxby Rob Robertson, John Badger, Brian Aves, Barry Downing, George Stewart and Mike Jones; seated, left to right, Howell Williams, Frank Brereton, Bob Barrass, Bev Brown, Cliff Downing Tony Jones and Tony Clare. (By courtesy of New Brighton RNLI)

Tractor TW1 brings the drive-on drive-off carriage down to the sea for recovery of the Atlantic 21. (By courtesy of New Brighton RNLI)

On 6 December 1983, with Helmsman Clifford Downing in command, B-549 *Blenwatch* was launched at 11am to stand by while the oil-rig *Sovereign Explorer* was launched from Cammell Laird shipyard. As the rig was being manoeuvred, one of the mooring lines parted, whipping back and severing the arm and part of the leg of one of the riggers on board. Lifeboat crew Mike Jones was put aboard the rig from the ILB and, with members of the boatyard's staff, applied tourniquets to the injured man and picked up the severed portion of his leg. The man and the portion of his leg, were put aboard the ILB and landed at Liverpool, where an ambulance was waiting. Lifeboat crew Frank Brereton watched the lines and debris in the water alongside the rig, and then assisted in getting the casualty and medics aboard. A Letter of Appreciation, signed by the RNLI's Chief of Operations, was sent to the New Brighton station, acknowledging the efforts done by all involved in what was a harrowing and extremely difficult task.

Presentation of Bronze medal certificate, Thanks on Vellum and Service Certificates at Wallasey Yacht Club following for the service to the yacht Ocea. Pictured, left to right, are: Dale Kaye, Thomas Baker, Edward 'Bev' Brown, Mike Jones and Lt Col R.N. Woosnam, who presented the certificates. (By courtesy of the RNLI)

After having delivered a load of stone to the site of the new beach-retention works, near the Perch Rock lighthouse, late on the morning of 26 September 1984, a lorry set off back along the causeway to the shore. But the causeway was covered by about 4ft of water from the incoming tide and, when the lorry was about half-way along the causeway, the tide pushed it sideways, the front near-side wheel slipped over the edge, and the lorry dropped onto its axle. The Coastguard was immediately informed and B-549 launched at 12.33pm to help. The lifeboatmen made their way round the lighthouse and through a gap between the new seawalls,

RNLI medal winners of 1982 at the the Annual Presentation of Awards in London on 17 May 1983. The lifeboatmen are, back row left to right, Coxswain Charles Hatcher (Blyth), Coxswain Hewitt Clarke (Lerwick), Edward 'Bev' Brown (New Brighton) and Robert Fossett (Southend-on-Sea); front row, left to right, Keirh Willecy (Morecambe), Eric Ward (St Ives), Alan Forrester (Flint) and Coxswain Michael Berry (St Helier). (By courtesy of New Brighton RNLI)

HRH The Duke of Kent presents Edward 'Bev' Brown with the Bronze medal for gallantry in London, May 1983. (By courtesy of New Brighton RNLI)

quickly got alongside the lorry and saved the driver, with the ILB landing him five minutes later.

At 5.40pm on 6 October 1987 B-549 *Blenwatch* was launched after a small yacht had been reported to be in difficulties just outside the main channel of the entrance to the Mersey, five miles north-west of New Brighton. Manned by Helmsman Anthony Clare and lifeboatmen Geoffrey Prince and Anthony Jones, the lifeboat headed for the reported position in steadily worsening conditions, squally showers reducing visibility, and began to search for the casualty. Once clear of the shelter of the land, they encountered short, steep seas with a 4ft swell and the westerly wind at force six. Nothing could be seen of the casualty and so Anthony Clare landed on a sandbank near the Training Wall and walked southwards, up to the highest point of the sandbank, to get a better view, but still nothing could be seen.

At this point, a Coastguard Officer at Hoylake managed to see the casualty, under way, heading in a south-westerly direction, south-west of the Burbo Bank. Anthony Clare rejoined his colleagues and the ILB set off at 6.30pm towards the new reported position. By the time they entered the Rock Channel, the wind had risen to force seven, gusting to gale force and it was getting dark. Seas up to 10ft in height were encountered in the Channel and, in view of the deteriorating conditions, Hoylake lifeboat *Mary Gabriel* was requested to be launch.

Launching the Atlantic 21 Blenwatch (B-549) in choppy seas. (By courtesy of New Brighton RNLI)

Helmsman Clare believed that, in the prevailing wind and sea conditions, the casualty would be driven back across the Burbo Bank and into the Main Channel, so he entered the Crosby Channel, the lifeboatmen searching as they went, despite the dark. Suddenly, at 7.25pm they spotted a vague shape and, by the light of a white parachute flare, saw the yacht aground on the Burbo Bank. She was being pounded by heavy, breaking seas and, in the deep troughs, the Training Wall could just be seen between yacht and lifeboat.

The crew of the yacht appeared to be trying to inflate a life-raft and Helmsman Clare realised that, if the yacht was driven onto the Training Wall, it would quickly break up. Carefully, he watched the wave pattern over the Wall and, choosing his moment, drove the Atlantic across the Wall. They got over safely but found the seas on the other side were very short, confused and breaking heavily due to the now gale-force wind and the reflected waves coming back off the Wall. The yacht was rolling heavily, with her boom swinging free, and so Helmsman Clare decided to try and tow the yacht back over the Training Wall and into the Main Channel, before attempting to rescue her crew of three.

He took the ILB in as close as he could to shout instructions across to the yachtsmen, while the other lifeboatmen prepared the tow line. The ILB was taken back in and crew member Geoffrey Prince, held in position in the ILB by Anthony Jones, passed the line across, with Helmsman Clare skilfully holding the ILB head-to-sea while the line was hauled in. Once it had been

Blenwatch (B-549), crewed by Helmsman Clifford Downing, Frank Brereton and F. Jones, alongside the rig Sovereign Explorer on 6 December 1983, preparing to take aboard the injured rigger. (By courtesy of Mike Jones)

Demolition of the first boathouse and preparation of the site for a new, larger boathouse, 1989. (By courtesy of New Brighton RNLI)

The lifeboat house completed in 1989 was much larger than the building it replaced and provided better crew facilities. (Nicholas Leach)

The lifeboat house on Kings Parade pictured in 1989 shortly after it had been completed. (Nicholas Leach)

secured, the yacht, the 24ft *Samsal*, was pulled round and towed over the Training Wall and into the Main Channel, at 7.50pm.

The yacht was pulled alongside the ILB so the lifeboat crew could check on the condition of the yachtsmen, who were all tired and wet, but bailing desperately as the yacht was leaking badly. They wanted to beach the yacht, but, in the prevailing conditions, no suitable beach was available so it was agreed to tow the yacht to Liverpool Marina. The tow up-channel was slow, with the yacht yawing wildly and the Coastguard was requested to arrange for the yacht to be received at the Marina, with the ILB and yacht arriving off the entrance to the Albert Dock complex at 8.45pm. Lifeboat crew Anthony Jones boarded the yacht which was secured alongside the Dock Wall, but as no lock into the Marina was available until the following morning Helmsman Clare decided to moor the yacht at Tranmere. However, the yacht's owner refused to move so, at 9.20pm, the ILB left the yacht, to return to station, the authorities having been made aware of the situation.

On the way back to station, the ILB's starboard engine failed and the recovery team were advised. They rigged the trolley for a net recovery, but conditions at the site were not good, with confused seas. Just as the ILB was approaching the recovery net, the net was carried away and the approach had to be aborted, while the net was re-rigged. At the second attempt, thanks to the excellent co-ordination with tractor driver Francis Brereton, B-549 was recovered safely at 9.45pm.

For his outstanding seamanship, courage and fine leadership, the RNLI's Thanks Inscribed on Vellum was accorded to Helmsman Anthony Clare. Framed Letters of Thanks, signed by the Chairman of the RNLI, were awarded to lifeboatmen Geoffrey Prince and Anthony Jones, with a Letter of Appreciation, signed by the Chief of Operations, going to tractor driver Francis Brereton.

In 1989 work started on a new lifeboat house, which was completed on the site of the first ILB house. The new house was considerably larger and provided improved crew facilities as well as room for a larger and more powerful launch vehicle. The new boathouse officially opened on 28 April 1990, with RNLI Divisional Inspector Mike Vlasto in attendance. A service of dedication was held, led by the Rev Anthony Jeynes, Chaplain of the station, after the formal opening of the building had been undertaken by the Mayor of Wirral Councillor Mike Cooke, who was also President of the station.

The lifeboat house built in 1989, pictured in February 1996. (Nicholas Leach)

On the morning of 22 December 1990 news was received that the 33ft fishing boat *Prospect* needed assistance, as her propeller had been fouled and her tiller broken. B-549 was launched at 10.22am and found the casualty in very shallow water over the North Bank. A very strong south-westerly wind was blowing, churning up very confused seas on the Bank and the fishing boat was repeatedly striking the bottom. The ILB was taken as close as possible and a tow line was passed across to the casualty and secured. Then, with waves washing over the ILB, the fishing boat was pulled clear of the sandbank and towed through the Rock Channel and into the Mersey. The boat was towed to Gladstone Docks, and B-549 returning to station at 12.35pm.

On the morning of 14 November 1993, in rough seas and a very strong northerly wind, the auxiliary-yacht *Traverse*, with two adults and two children on board, got into difficulties off Eastham Locks, eight and a half miles from New Brighton. The crew were unable to hoist sail and the auxiliary engine was not powerful enough to cope with the prevailing wind and sea conditions. B-549 was launched at 8.56am and, on reaching the yacht, the skipper requested that the two children be taken off. But, in the prevailing conditions, Helmsman Barrass considered it would be safer if the children remained on board the yacht and one of the lifeboatmen went aboard to help. A tow line was secured to the yacht, which was towed to Liverpool Marina, with the tow parting once during the passage. It was quickly reconnected and the two boats reached the Marina safely. The ILB remained afloat in the river until the

Lifeboat crew on board Blenwatch (B-549) outside the lifeboat house with, left to right, DLA Frank Brereton, Chairman Eric Lowe, Honorary Secretary Phil Hockey, DLA Peter Wilson, Mike Garbutt, Dave Williams, Tony Jones, Bob Marr and Stewart Ward. (By courtesy of New Brighton RNLI)

tide had dropped and she was able to return to station and beached safely, at 12.45pm. This had been a long, demanding service, in bitterly cold weather and the lifeboat crew members were very cold and tired on their return to station.

On 14 April 1994 news was received at 7.15am that a young trainee was missing overboard from the sail training ship *Malcolm Miller*, which was seven miles north-west of the Bar Lanby in choppy seas and a fresh north-westerly wind. Seven minutes later Relief Atlantic 21 *Ernest Armstrong* (B-592) was launched, manned by Senior Helmsman Robert Barrass, Helmsman Anthony Clare and lifeboatmen John Badger and Neil Jones. They reached the training ship at 8.20am and made a thorough search of the immediate area. The on-scene commander was Captain Robert Joss, of the oil survey vessel *Grampian Eagle* and, at his request, the lifeboatmen joined other vessels, including the Lytham St Annes lifeboat *Sarah Emily Harrop*, in a wider search pattern. This continued until some of the vessels were released by the Coastguard, while the Hoylake lifeboat *Lady of Hilbre* joined the search, the Hoylake crew providing some welcome hot drinks for New Brighton's lifeboatmen.

With RAF and Police helicopters involved, the search continued but sadly without success, during which some much needed fuel was supplied to New Brighton lifeboat by *Grampian Eagle*. At 1pm, with no sign of the missing trainee and conditions steadily worsening, the Atlantic was recalled, arriving back at New Brighton at 2pm. The RNLI's Chief of Operations later sent a Letter of Thanks to the Honorary Secretary in appreciation of this fine service and the devotion to duty in very uncomfortable

Atlantic 21 Blenwatch (B-549) greets the Cunard liner Queen Elizabeth 2 as the ship visits the Mersey on her farewell tour in 2007. (By courtesy of New Brighton RNLI)

conditions carried out by Senior Helmsman Barrass, Helmsman Anthony Clare and lifeboatmen John Badger and Neil Jones. The Chief of Operations also sent a Letter of Thanks to Captain Robert Joss, of *Grampian Eagle*, congratulating him on the way in which he had carried out his duties and thanking him in particular for the help he had given to the New Brighton lifeboat.

Shortly before midnight on 7 June 1994 the Coastguard requested the ILB be launched, after a vehicle had apparently smashed through the railings on the Promenade opposite Kingslake Road, Egremont, a very steep hill. Relief Atlantic 21 *Ernest Armstrong* (B-592), which was still on station, was launched at 11.55pm and, once she was away, the other crew members formed a shore party and hurried round to the scene by road. The Police and Fire Brigade were also sent, as was the Liverpool County Rescue Boat and, as the Fire Brigade set up extra lighting, RNLI shore helper and former lifeboat crew Tony Jones got a rope ladder from a Fire Engine, lowered it over the nearby railings and secured it to provided safe entry into the water below. Crew members Mike Jones and Tony Clare took off their outer-clothes and entered the water, just as the ILB arrived on the scene.

The water was about 10ft deep and it was believed that the vehicle was about 30ft out from the sea wall. Mike Jones and Tony Clare repeatedly dived down, to try and locate the vehicle, while two firemen, wearing breathing apparatus, also entered the water to help with the search. But, as they were not trained divers and their equipment made it difficult for them to swim, they were recalled by their Senior Officer. Meanwhile the crew of the ILB, under Senior Helmsman Bob Barrass, was also searching the area using their echo-sounder and they located the car. Mike Jones was able to get on top of the vehicle, which was lying upside down, and

Relief Atlantic 21 B-533 on service to a man who got washed into the sea just to the north of the lifeboat station, with the County Rescue ILB standing by, 5 March 1995. (By courtesy of the RNLI)

attached a Fire Brigade rope to the axle. The car was then pulled closer to the seawall, turning onto its side in the process.

Mike Jones opened the vehicle's back door, helped by lifeboat crew Mike Garbutt on the ILB. Tony Clare then dived down, felt around inside the car and pulled the occupant clear with the help of Mike Jones, onto the ILB. He was a big man and, with his clothes holding so much water, it was very difficult to get him aboard the lifeboat. But, while Tony Clare and Mike Jones dived back down to the car, to ensure that no one else was inside, the crew of the ILB hauled the man aboard. Mouth-to-mouth resuscitation and heart-massage was immediately started by crew members Neil Jones and Barry Shillinglaw, with Mike Garbutt monitoring the man's pulse and co-ordinating the efforts, the whole procedure being extremely unpleasant for everyone involved.

Relief Atlantic 21 B-533 returns from service on 5 March 1995 with Mike Jones on the helm. (By courtesy of the RNLI)

On board relief Atlantic 21 B-533 after the service on 5 March 1995 are, left to right, Michael Haxby, Mike Jones, Howard Jones and Neil Jones. (By courtesy of the RNLI)

Helmsman Barrass shouted to those ashore that he would beach the ILB on the Egremont Slip, 200 yards away and immediate medical assistance at that slipway was requested. The ILB was duly beached and the casualty was lifted out of the boat and laid on the ground. Shore helper Tony Jones took over heart massage, with the resuscitation efforts continuing until the ambulance arrived two minutes later. Once the paramedics had taken over, the ILB crew and shore helpers assisted as much as possible with resuscitation efforts continuing for a further fifteen minutes. The man was then placed in the ambulance and rushed to hospital. The ILB was manually relaunched and returned to station at 1.10am. Sadly, despite the efforts by everyone involved, the man later died.

For their outstanding bravery, courage and utter determination, Mike Jones and Anthony Clare were accorded the Thanks Inscribed on Vellum. For the determined and valiant efforts they made in trying to resuscitate the man, and for the important part they played, Framed Letters of Thanks, signed by the Chairman of the RNLI, were awarded to Neil Jones, Barry Shillinglaw and Tony Jones. Letters of Thanks, signed by the Director of the RNLI, were sent to Helmsman Bob Barrass and crew member Mike Garbutt, and also to shore helpers Stuart Ward, Arne Jensen, Eric Stancliffe and Bob Marr, for the excellent support they gave during this extremely traumatic service.

Atlantic 21 B-549 Blenwatch launching on exercise at high water. Talus 4WH tractor TW17H was the second such vehicle to serve the station, from 1990 to 1996. (Jeff Morris)

While Helmsman Mike Jones was in the boathouse at 2pm on 5 March 1995, he was informed by a member of the public, that a man was in the sea trying to rescue his dog, which had been swept off Portland Slip just to the north of the lifeboat station. Five minutes later, the Relief Atlantic 21 B-533 was launched through heavy surf, manned by Helmsman Jones and Howard Jones, Neil Jones and Michael Haxby. In rough seas and a westerly gale, the ILB passed through the Rock Channel, where waves up to 20ft high were encountered. Onlookers ashore later reported that, on at least two occasions, the ILB came completely clear of the water.

The County Rescue ILB, a 6.5m rigid-inflatable, manned by Sub-Officer Richard Finlay and John Goodwin, who were already on service in the area, was diverted to the scene and reached the man first, finding him about fifty yards offshore lying face down in the water. The two men in the County Rescue boat tried desperately to pull him aboard their boat, which nearly capsized twice in the rough seas. The lifeboat reached the scene two minutes later and the crew began to try and recover the man. Lifeboatman Howard Jones grabbed hold of him and passed him to Neil Jones but the ILB was picked up on the crest of a wave and Neil Jones, who did not let go of the casualty, was dragged overboard by the weight of the man. However, he then managed to pass the man's arm to Michael Haxby, who pulled the man further aft, while Neil Jones managed to get back on board. The man was 6ft 4in tall and weighed eighteen stones, his wet clothes adding to his weight, and trying to pull him aboard the ILB took the combined efforts of all three lifeboatmen.

Atlantic 21 B-549 Blenwatch on exercise. She was on station from 1981 to 1996, and then served at various other stations before being sold by the RNLI having given more than two decades of service. She was one of a handful of Atlantic 21 ILBs to be fitted with a windscreen, which offered a degree of protection for the three crew. (Jeff Morris)

Resuscitation efforts began immediately by all three crew members, while Helmsman Jones headed through the Rock Channel. In order to help his colleagues with their attempts to revive the man, he kept the speed down to only about seven knots, but, in the very bad conditions, the casualty and crew were constantly swamped. Twice, a net recovery of the ILB was attempted but had to be called off because the trolley was repeatedly shifting in the rough seas, so Helmsman Jones made for Egremont, where the shore party headed by road. Eventually, the ILB was recovered safely on the Egremont Slip, and the combined efforts of all four lifeboatmen were needed to get the man ashore, where he was handed into the care of ambulance men. They spent fifteen minutes working on the man, before taking him to hospital, where, sadly, he was pronounced dead on arrival. The ILB was relaunched and returned to station at 4.15pm.

For this difficult service, the RNLI's Thanks Inscribed on Vellum was accorded to Helmsman Mike Jones, with Framed Letters of Appreciation, signed by the Chairman of the Institution, going to lifeboatmen Howard Jones, Neil Jones and Michael Haxby. The crew of the County Rescue Boat, Sub-Officer Richard Finlay and crew member John Goodwin, were also awarded Framed Letters of Thanks signed by the Chairman of the RNLI. The RNLI's Director later sent Letters of Thanks to shore helpers Francis Brereton, R. Marr, S. Ward, A. Jones and Peter Shillinglaw in recognition of their very considerable efforts that day.

During the last few months of her career at New Brighton, Atlantic 21 B-549 continued to undertake some fine rescues, with another coming on 4 June 1995. She was launched at 5.28pm to the aid of the fishing boat *Polly*, with five people on board, which had broken down seven miles off New Brighton, in rough seas and a strong north-westerly wind. The ILB towed the disabled boat to Liverpool Marina, where the boat was moored to await the next tide to enter the Marina. But the skipper of the fishing boat was a diabetic and needed to get medication from his car. He had only one leg and it was with great difficulty that he was taken aboard the ILB. Helmsman Bob Barrass then remembered that the sail training vessel *Lord Nelson*, belonging to the Jubilee Sailing Trust which assists physically handicapped people enjoy sailing, was moored alongside the Prince's Landing Stage and so he went alongside the vessel, explained the problem and asked for help in landing the disabled man. Although the crew were eating at the time, everyone immediately stopped and quickly rigged a special hoist to lift the man aboard and he was then put ashore to get the medication that he needed, while the ILB returned to station at 6.30pm. The RNLI's Deputy Chief of Operations later sent a Letter of Thanks to the Master of *Lord Nelson* for the help that he and his crew had provided.

B-721 Rock Light

On 9 January 1996, a new Atlantic 75 was placed on station. The new craft was a far cry from the early days of the Atlantic 21 more than twenty years ago. The 75, first developed during the early 1990s, was fitted with twin 70hp Evinrude outboards, which gave a top speed of thirty-two knots. Sufficient fuel was carried for three hours' operation at full speed, giving a range of approximately thirty-five miles, which could be extended considerably when speed was moderated. Two water ballast tanks were fitted in the bow and these, together with the trim/tilt engine mechanism, provided the crew with full control of the trim in any sea conditions. The hull shape had been modified from the Atlantic 21 to give a smoother ride, while the sponsons had been enlarged.

The new ILB, B-721, which had cost £76,250 to build, was funded from an appeal by the

Countess of Derby formally names the Atlantic 75 Rock Light (B-721) on 11 May 1996 at the Old Pier. (By courtesy of New Brighton RNLI)

Port and City of Liverpool Branch of the RNLI and local efforts by the New Brighton station. She was named *Rock Light* after the lighthouse at the entrance to the Mersey and in appreciation of all the help and support given to the RNLI by the people of Merseyside. The new lifeboat was formally named at a ceremony on 11 May 1996 at the site of the Old Pier. The Rt Hon The Earl of Derby, patron of the Port and City of Liverpool Branch, handed the lifeboat over to Anthony Hannay, a member of the committee of management who accepted it on behalf of the RNLI, who in turn passed it into the safekeeping of the station. Following a service of dedication, the new lifeboat was named by the Countess of Derby and the boat was then launched for a short demonstration run in the Mersey.

Rock Light (B-721) was operated at New Brighton for almost fourteen years, giving outstanding service, saving many lives and performing some fine rescues, proving to be an excellent rescue tool for her volunteer crews. Her first rescue took place on 20 April 1996, when she landed a sick man from the tanker *Saint Kearan*. The tanker was not typical of the kind of casualties to which *Rock Light (B-721)* was mostly called, as the great majority of her calls were to yachts, jet skis, powerboats and various other

Below left: Earl Lord Derby, the Mayor and Mayoress of Wirral tak to Senior Helmsman Robert Barrass after the naming of Rock Light on 11 May 1996.

Below right: Mike Jones, Graham Lowe and Senior Helmsman Robert Barrass on board Rock Light (B-721) after her naming on 11 May 1996. (Photos by courtesy of New Brighton RNLI)

Atlantic 75 Rock Light (B-721) launching on exercise on 25 February 1996, just over a month after being placed on station. (Nicholas Leach)

pleasure craft. In June 1999, having spent three busy years at New Brighton, she was taken away for a refit at the RNLI's Inshore Lifeboat Centre in Cowes, and in her place came the relief Atlantic 75 *Walters Lifeboat* (B-723), which remained until January 2000, and which was involved in another noteworthy service.

In the early hours of Christmas Day 1999 Liverpool Coastguard reported that two people were in the sea at Victoria Slip, New Brighton. Conditions were extremely bad, with a north-westerly gale gusting to forty-seven knots was causing very heavy, confused

Atlantic 75 Rock Light (B-721) being brought down onto the beach for an exercise launch. (Nicholas Leach)

Atlantic 75 Rock Light (B-721) launching on exercise, February 1996. (Nicholas Leach)

Atlantic 75 Rock Light (B-721) heads out into the Mersey on exercise in February 1996. Part of Liverpool's dock complexes can be seen in the backgrdound. (Nicholas Leach)

seas, with waves up to 10ft high. Honorary Secretary Frank Brereton advised the immediate launch of Hoylake lifeboat *Lady of Hilbre* while he assessed the situation at New Brighton. With Helmsman Mike Jones, he was taken by the tractor to check possible launch sites as the usual one was not usable because of the dreadful conditions. They decided that the ILB could be safely launched at the Fort Slipway, where there was some protection from the confused seas. Although conditions were in excess of the operating limits for the Atlantic, Frank agreed to the launch as the ILB would be operating in an area which did offer a partial lee and the scene was well lit from the shore.

Three experienced lifeboatmen, Howard Jones, Barry Shillinglaw and Paul Wright, went with Helmsman Mike Jones, and the extra man was taken because of the nature of the call. And so, at

Atlantic 75 Rock Light (B-721) on exercise in February 1996, a month after being placed on station. (Nicholas Leach)

12.53am *Walters Lifeboat* (B-723) was launched at the Fort Slipway into heavy, very confused seas, facing waves up to 10ft high. The lifeboatmen reached the reported position, half-a-mile away, in just five minutes and immediately began a search of the area, which was lit by car headlights, torches and searchlights, as shore helpers from the station joined Police, Coastguards and members of the public on the Promenade. Just after 1am one man was recovered ashore and this information was radioed to the lifeboatmen. A few minutes later, a Police helicopter arrived and shone its powerful searchlight onto the area.

B-723 headed towards the Fort, keeping close inshore, battling exceptionally rough seas up to 15ft high near the Promenade Wall. At 1.20am the lifeboatmen spotted a lifebuoy 200 yards offshore and went to investigate, as it had been thrown from the Promenade to the men in the water. The lifebuoy was pulled aboard the ILB by Barry Shillinglaw, who realised that the lanyard was attached to something. So he hauled in the rest of the line, and the body of the second man surfaced. The three lifeboatmen managed to pull the waterlogged casualty aboard the ILB and radioed this to the Coastguard, stating that there appeared to be no sign of life as the man had been in the water for well over half an hour.

Helmsman Jones was now faced with the problem of where to beach the ILB so as to land the casualty as quickly as possible, while the three crew began efforts to resuscitate the man. Helmsman Jones decided that the Egremont South Slip was the only possible safe beaching site and so headed there, with the wind having risen to fifty knots. On reaching the slip, the crew held the casualty steady ready to disembark him on beaching, and the man was

Atlantic 75 Rock Light (B-721) outside the lifeboat house on the hoist used to turn the boat round after a net recovery. (By courtesy of New Brighton RNLI)

handed over to paramedics who rushed him to hospital, where, sadly, he was pronounced dead on arrival. The ILB was relaunched and had to remain afloat while the tide dropped sufficiently to enable her to be recovered.

Meanwhile, the Hoylake lifeboat, which had made best speed possible to the site despite the atrocious conditions, arrived at 1.42am and gave the New Brighton lifeboatmen some much needed hot drinks. At 2.10am after the ILB had been recovered at the Egremont North Slip, the Hoylake lifeboat set off back to her station, her crew having a particularly rough trip in the exceptionally heavy, confused seas, the worst that some of the crew had ever experienced. But they reached Hoylake safely and the lifeboat was beached at 3.04am.

Andy Hurley, Deputy Divisional Inspector of Lifeboats, made the following observations in his official report of this service:

'Mr Brereton made extremely difficult decisions in selecting the crew and launching the lifeboat at the very limit of its operational capabilities. These decisions were supported by all involved in the service. The boathandling, seamanship and leadership of Helmsman Jones were outstanding, particularly during the launch and initial beaching. The search was well executed in the severe conditions. The other crew members performed very well in adverse weather, displaying courage and determination. The shore helpers also contributed greatly to the service and undoubtedly kept the damage to the lifeboat at the time of beaching, to a minimum. The Hoylake lifeboat crew provided great comfort to the New Brighton crew by being there. The

Atlantic 75 Rock Light (B-721) with Hoylake lifeboat Lady of Hilbre (on left) and West Kirby D class inflatable inshore lifeboat Thomas Jefferson (D-473) in the Mersey in March 1999 to mark the 175th anniversary of the founding of the RNLI. (By courtesy of New Brighton RNLI)

A historic meeting as Atlantic 75 Rock Light (B-721) goes alongside the station's former lifeboat, the 60ft Barnett William and Kate Johnston, during the Mersey River Festival in June 2002. (Nicholas Leach)

Rock Light (B-721) and the station's former 60ft Barnett William and Kate Johnston in the Mersey during the River Festival, June 2002. (Nicholas Leach)

Below: Rock Light (B-721) on duty during the Mersey River Festival, June 2002. (Nicholas Leach)

return passage to Hoylake was in the worst seas that some of the crew had encountered.'

For his outstanding seamanship, excellent boathandling and fine leadership during this service, Helmsman Mike Jones was awarded the Thanks on Vellum by the RNLI. For their courage and determination, Framed Letters of Thanks signed by the Chairman of the RNLI were awarded to lifeboatmen Howard Jones, Barry Shillinglaw and Paul Wright. The shore helpers had all played a major part in this extremely demanding service, especially when the casualty was landed and the ILB was later relaunched, and they each received a Letter of Appreciation signed by the RNLI's Chief of Operations. They were Neil Jones, Nigel Jones, Christopher Henderson, Ian Thornton, Simon Bowers, Paul Mountford, Mark Harding and Anthony Clare.

A Letter of Appreciation, signed by the RNLI's Chief of Operations, was sent to Honorary Secretary Frank Brereton, who had made some extremely challenging decisions, including agreeing to launch the lifeboat at the very limit of its operational capabilities. A Letter of Appreciation, signed by the Chief of Operations, was also sent to the Coxswain and crew of the Hoylake lifeboat for their help and support, as the New Brighton crew had taken great comfort in the knowledge that the Hoylake lifeboat was on its way to help.

Rock Light (B-721) returned in early 2000 and the first year of the new millennium proved to be a very busy one, with yachts, motor boats and jet skis all being helped. The following year was another busy one, and among the many services performed was

Rock Light (B-721) in the Mersey in May 2003 for the Battle of Atlantic 60th Anniversary commemorations. (Nicholas Leach)

one on 19 October 2001, to a pleasure boat, which was reported to have run aground three and a half miles from New Brighton, and *Rock Light* (B-721) was launched at 7pm to investigate. In rapidly fading light, the lifeboatmen could find no sign of the casualty and, after searching for a while without success, they thought it had been a hoax. But they continued, illuminating the area with parachute flares and, eventually, the casualty was spotted, high and dry on a sandbank.

She was the 10m cabin cruiser *Tomelou*, with two men on board, which had run aground after suffering engine failure. As the ILB was unable to get near her, she went to the back of the sandbank where the lifeboatmen waited for the flood tide. The cabin cruiser eventually refloated and was then towed to Liverpool Marina by the ILB, with the boats arriving there at 11pm. The Coastguard then radioed the lifeboatmen asking them to go to Otterpool, six miles south-east of New Brighton, where the Fire Brigade were trying to help a very distressed dog owner rescue the animal from the water. Guided to the scene by the Fire Brigade, the ILB was quickly on the spot, rescued the dog and reunited the animal with its very grateful owner.

Over the weekend of 15-16 June 2002 New Brighton lifeboat station took an active part in the Liverpool River Festival, with *Rock Light* (B-721) on the water to take part in a parade of boats. Perhaps the main attraction of the event was the station's former lifeboat, *William and Kate Johnston*, which had returned to the Mersey for the first time since leaving the station in September 1950. Also on hand on 16 June was Hoylake lifeboat *Lady of Hilbre*, with which an RAF Rescue helicopter performed a demonstration airlift for the benefit of the large crowd that lined Liverpool's historic waterfront. *William and Kate Johnston* led the parade of sail in the afternoon, in which hundreds of craft small and large sailed into the Mersey out of Liverpool's historic Albert Dock.

One of the most noteworthy rescues carried out using *Rock Light* (B-721) took place on 18 April 2005 after the 7m cabin cruiser *Melody*, with four people on board, got into difficulty in deteriorating weather conditions in the approaches to the Mersey. Two of the four had been washed overboard. Manned by Helmsman Mark Bland, Mark Harding as Radio Operator and Greg Morgan as crew, *Rock Light* (B-721) launched at around midday to begin searching for the two men who had gone overboard. As the lifeboat headed north-west, the wind against tide gave the crew an uncomfortable ride. The sea state was rough with large, white breaking waves in the shallows over the Great Burbo Bank and waves of approximately 4m in the channel, and visibility was very poor due to the amount of spray being thrown up by the lifeboat.

Further offshore conditions were worse, with bigger waves and wind speeds in excess of thirty knots, but according to Helmsman Bland, 'the ILB was fabulous, phenomenally capable'. The lifeboat crew made their way as safely as the conditions allowed, with the lifeboat often travelling at less than twelve knots, but they reached Melody at around 12.15pm. As the lifeboat approached, the crew were told that the two men overboard had been recovered. The skipper had not lost sight of them and had been able to retrieve them. The vessel was slowly heading towards Liverpool for shelter, so crew member Mark Harding was transferred onto the cabin cruiser, at the second attempt, facing a deck littered with fishing equipment.

Hoylake all-weather lifeboat *Lady of Hilbre* had launched to help, while on board *Melody* Mark reported that the two rescued men were suffering from the effects of the cold and one had sustained a neck or shoulder injury. Both were placed in the wheelhouse and stabilised. The lifeboat's first aid kit and oxygen were transferred onto the casualty while *Melody's* skipper continued to tackle the large following seas. Conditions on board *Melody* were horrendous and the more seriously injured man began to deteriorate quickly.

Atlantic 75 Rock Light (B-721) in the Mersey for the Tall Ships Parade of Sail on 21 July 2008. (Nicholas Leach)

Rock Light (B-721) in the Mersey for the Tall Ships gathering on 21 July 2008, with crowds lining the Birkenhead shore to see the ships parade down the river. (Nicholas Leach)

The boats were still about six miles from the Mersey in deteriorating weather, with one man needing urgent medical assistance. *Melody* was only managing to make four to five knots towards Liverpool, the all-weather lifeboat was up to an hour away and the Rescue 122 helicopter was not available. Helmsman Mark Bland explained what happened next:

'First, I directed Crew Member Greg Morgan to also transfer to assist Mark. They fitted a cervical collar to the injured man, placed a survival bag around him and administered oxygen therapy. I witnessed Melody broach severely on several occasions, which must have been how the guys got washed out in the first place. At one point I saw the propeller of their boat and half the hull.

Atlantic 75 Rock Light (B-721) seen form the air during an exercise with RAF Rescue helicopter, with the helicopter winchman holding onto the lifeboat's helm console while undertaking crew transfers. (Mike Jones)

Below: Atlantic 75 Rock Light (B-721) and hovercraft Hurley Spirit (H-005) exercising with RAF Rescue helicopter from Valley; this was the first joint ILB and hovercraft exercise with the helicopter. (Simon Clitheroe, courtesy of Mike Jones)

Concerned for their own safety and that of the casualty vessel, Mark Harding took the controls of Melody with the skipper's blessing while Greg monitored and reassured both of the immersion victims.

'I decided to make towards the Pier Head, Liverpool. With Melody now making around ten to twelve knots, she became much more stable and made good progress. County Rescue [River Mersey Inshore Rescue boat] met with us and both boats escorted Melody down the Crosby Channel. After about thirty minutes, extra oxygen was passed to us and then to Melody. One

of the County Rescue crew, also an RNLI crew member from Hoylake, transferred to assist me in the B class.'

County Rescue departed to make preparations at the Pier Head to transfer the men to the waiting paramedics, while Hoylake lifeboat reached the scene and stood by. Crew member Mark Harding berthed *Melody* alongside County Rescue and the injured men was brought safely ashore at around 2pm. The lifeboat crew rejoined the lifeboat and headed back to New Brighton, where the lifeboat was recovered and taken back to station to refuel. The lifeboat was back ready for service at 2.52pm. Helmsman Mark Bland concluded his account:

'After the shout we were all exhausted from getting such a battering on the way out. My arms felt like they'd been pulled out of their sockets. Throughout this demanding service the performance of the lifeboat and my crew was exemplary. All I did was get them there. Without them, those we rescued would have been in a far worse condition.'

RNLI Chairman Admiral Sir Jock Slater sent letters of appreciation to the crew, saying: 'Your teamwork and determination in the most testing conditions that afternoon were in the best traditions of the RNLI. Well done!'

Another unusual incident occurred on 11 July 2009 during a visit to the lifeboat station by the Mayor of Wirral, Cllr Andrew Hodson, when the volunteer crew were paged to attend a rescue. The boathouse was full of people, including the Mayor and Mayoress of Wirral as part of an open weekend, and they were able to see exactly what happens to prepare the boat and the crew

Net recovery at the Fort slipway of Atlantic 75 Rock Light (B-721) after a rough weather exercise, to practice launching and net recovery, with Dave Hicks on the helm. (Mike Jones)

Atlantic 75 Rock Light (B-721) breaks through a wave as she launches. This rough weather exercise involved a launch south of New Brighton Pier with Paul Mountford on the helm. (Mike Jones)

to go to sea. A leisure boat had lost power in the channel and was going the wrong way. There were four people on board who were unharmed but very pleased to receive assistance. The vessel was towed and then passed to the Hoylake lifeboat to continue so the Atlantic 75 crew could return to the open day. Cllr Andrew Hodson, Mayor of Wirral said:

'I really enjoyed my visit to RNLI New Brighton Lifeboat station and meeting the volunteer crews and their families. The service that they provide is absolutely vital to the people of Wirral and beyond and that's why the RNLI is one of my chosen charities this year. As the boat went to sea I stayed and chatted to some of the fund-raising volunteers. Seeing the crew in action was absolutely fantastic!'

This was one of the last services performed by *Rock Light* (B-721) during her busy career at New Brighton. She was replaced by a new lifeboat in November 2009 and, after a few months in the Relief Fleet, was sold out of service by the RNLI to ICE-SAR, the Icelandic lifeboat service. She was shipped over to Iceland, entered service with ICE-SAR and continued her life-saving career.

B-837 Charles Dibdin

On 10 November 2009 a new Atlantic 85, number B-837, arrived at New Brighton and was placed on station the following day after crew training and familiarisation had been completed. The Atlantic 85 was developed during the early years of the twenty-first century, and was intended to replace the old Atlantic 21 and 75 lifeboats, which had given such good service. The 85 was larger than B-721 *Rock Light*, at 8.3m in length, and had seating for a fourth crew member, and also carried more electronic equipment, including a radar and VHF direction finder. Powered by twin 115hp four-stroke engines and with a hull built from carbon composite, the 85 had a top speed of thirty-five knots, with an endurance of two and a

Atlantic 85 Charles Dibdin (Civil Service No.51) (B-837) on exercise in the Mersey in November 2009, with Mike Jones on the helm, a few days after being placed on station. (Nicholas Leach)

Charles Dibdin (Civil Service No.51) (B-837) on exercise in the Mersey with Hoylake's 12m Mersey lifeboat Lady of Hilbre. (Nicholas Leach)

Charles Dibdin (Civil Service No.51) (B-837) on exercise in the Mersey in November 2009. (Nicholas Leach)

half hours, and is equipped with intercom for easy communication.

The new Atlantic 85 for New Brighton, which cost £160,000, was named *Charles Dibdin (Civil Service No.51)* having been funded by The Communications and Public Servant Lifeboat Fund. The boat was the 51st to be provided by The Lifeboat Fund, a charity of the Civil Service, Royal Mail and BT. Sir Kevin Tebbitt, chairman of the Fund, said: 'We are delighted to be able to continue our long tradition of funding lifeboats throughout the UK for the Royal National Lifeboat Institution. The new Atlantic 85 lifeboat is named after the founder of the Lifeboat Fund, Charles Dibdin,

who started it in 1866 with an appeal to colleagues to raise £300 for a new lifeboat. He would be very proud that the Lifeboat Fund is still supporting the charity, and so it is only fitting that New Brighton's new lifeboat should bear his name.'

B-837 was formally named *Charles Dibdin (Civil Service No.51)* at a ceremony held on 24 July 2010, with Diana Allpress, Honorary Secretary of The Lifeboat Fund, christening the boat. More than 200 people gathered in Victoria Gardens on Marine Promenade for the occasion, during which a service of dedication was led by the Reverend Canon Frank Cain of St James Church. Frank Brereton, Chairman of New Brighton RNLI Lifeboat Management Group, said: 'We are extremely grateful to the members of the Lifeboat Fund for their continued support. We are absolutely thrilled with *Charles Dibdin*. With her increased speed and size and advances like radar, the Atlantic 85 enables our volunteer lifeboat crew to carry out their life saving work more safely and effectively than ever before'. Diana Allpress, Honorary Secretary of the Fund, added: 'We are delighted to be able to continue our long tradition of funding lifeboats for the RNLI, of which the Lifeboat Fund remains the single largest supporter'. At the end of the ceremony

The lifeboat crew line up for the naming ceremony of Charles Dibdin (Civil Service No.51) (B-837) on 24 July 2010. (Bob Warwick)

Lifeboat crew on board Charles Dibdin (Civil Service No.51) (B-837) for her naming ceremony on 24 July 2010. (Martin Fish)

The naming ceremony of Charles Dibdin (Civil Service No.51) (B-837) on 24 July 2010 at Victoria Gardens, Floral Pavilion, New Brighton with Mrs Diana Allpress (on right) about to pour the champagne over the boat's bows. (Martin Fish)

Mrs Diana Allpress formally names Charles Dibdin (Civil Service No.51) (B-837) on 24 July 2010 at Victoria Gardens, Floral Pavilion. (Martin Fish)

Charles Dibdin (Civil Service No.51) (B-837) being launched at the end of her naming ceremony on 24 July 2010. (Martin Fish)

B-837 Charles Dibdin (Civil Service No.51) being launched at the end of her naming ceremony on 24 July 2010. (Martin Fish)

the lifeboat was launched and put through her paces for the benefit of the gathered crowd of supporters and well-wishers.

Since being placed on station, B–837 has undertaken many services, continuing the fine tradition of life-saving on the Mersey that was established almost 150 years prior to her arrival. The lifeboat had been called out several times before her official naming, including working with Hoylake lifeboat on 11 June 2010 to assist a stricken yacht. The 34ft yacht, which was on passage from Douglas in the Isle of Man to Liverpool with three persons on board, became disabled after its steering gear failed.

Liverpool Coastguard tasked Hoylake and New Brighton lifeboats to help the casualty, which was drifting in the Crosby Channel approach to the port. B–837 was first on scene and a crew member was put aboard as the lifeboat took the vessel in tow. The casualty was in the middle of the Mersey and there was a significant amount of traffic in the river at the time. The weather was north-westerly force six to seven, and in the difficult conditions the tow line parted. By then Hoylake lifeboat *Lady of Hilbre*, under the command of

Charles Dibdin (Civil Service No.51) (B-837) being brought back to the boathouse on her carriage. Negotiating the traffic on the often busy Promenade can be a tricky task for the station's launchers and shore crew. (Martin Fish)

Lifeboat crew and station personnel with Charles Dibdin (Civil Service No.51) (B-837) and hovercraft Hurley Spirit (H-005) on the beach. (Bob Warwick)

Coxswain Dave Whiteley, had arrived on scene, and the Hoylake crew made fast a tow rope, with the assistance of the New Brighton crew member on board the yacht, which was towed to the safety of Liverpool Marina. With the yacht safe, Hoylake lifeboat returned to station at 1.10am on 12 June 2010 while New Brighton lifeboat was tasked to another incident further up the Mersey.

In April 2013 John Earp, the longest serving member of New Brighton station, received The Wirral Award for his outstanding and distinguished service to the people of Wirral at a ceremony conducted by the Mayor of Wirral Councillor Gerry Ellis. John's lifeboat career started in 1973, just as the Atlantic 21 ILBs were being introduced. He was a local yachtsman and member of Wallasey Yacht Club and became a Deputy Launching Authority, coordinating many of the early rescues with B-509, while also involved in fund-raising efforts and other aspects of the station's operation. Frank Brereton Chairman of RNLI New Brighton commented: 'John has been a stalwart of the station for the last 40 years and this award is well deserved. It's also appropriate as this year sees the 40th anniversary of the introduction of the B Class Atlantic series of rapid response lifeboats'.

RNLI 150th anniversary vellum presented to the station in 2012.

On 22 July 2013 B-837 Charles Dibdin was launched at 12.20pm to assist a 60ft yacht with a crew of three that was aground on the groyne off New Brighton lighthouse. The tide was going out and the sea was fairly calm when the lifeboat launched. Also on the scene were the beach lifeguard jet-ski and MF&RS Marine Rescue Unit's craft. Helmsman Dave Hicks recalled events:

'When we saw the craft, which was lying at an acute angle, we estimated that we had about ten minutes to get it afloat. When we arrived, two lifeguards were on board along with the yacht's crew. We put crewman Stuart Ward on board and set up a tow from its stern, while the Marine Rescue team put a line on its bow. We managed to tow it stern first off the groyne and then Marine

Rescue pulled its bow round and towed it out of the danger zone to the relief of all concerned.'

The yacht headed for Langton Dock under her own power, but the engines started to overheat so B-837 resumed the tow, with Marine Rescue providing extra stability. Summing up, Dave said: 'This was a team effort by all the agencies involved. We had to work quickly together with no room for error and we achieved a good result as the outcome for the yacht could have been very different if it had remained aground. Our own crew did exceptionally well and our training really paid off'.

The 150th anniversary of the founding of the station was celebrated during 2013 as the station had been founded in 1863. The first event to celebrate the 150th anniversary was a dinner dance at the Leasowe Castle Hotel attended by 140 dignitaries, lifeboat and fund-raising volunteers from New Brighton and Hoylake. During the event, senior helmsman Dave Lowe told the story of one of the station's significant rescues, to the French steamer *Emile Delmas* in the early hours of 24 November 1928, when the crew of *William*

Lifeboat crew and station personnel, past and present, gather for the station's 150th anniversary dinner at Leasowe Castle Hotel in January 2013. (Bob Warwick)

Charles Dibdin (Civil Service No.51) (B-837) being taken along the Promenade during the flooding that hit New Brighton on 5 December 2013, with the lifeboat house ending up 2ft deep in water. The lifeboat and tractor went along the Promenade, which was several feet under water in places, to check the hovercraft building. On the return, the lifeboat volunteers helped evacuate several families from the Bubble Playworld. Driving the tractor was Mike Jones, and on the boat were Ian Thornton (DLA) and Mike Plaskett. (Mike Jones)

and Kate Johnston saved twenty-four lives. To complete the evening RNLI Council member Anthony Hannay presented to Lifeboat Operations Manager Graham Sale a Vellum signed by HRH The Duke of Kent, President of the RNLI.

On Sunday 22 June 2014 both Atlantic 85 and hovercraft (see next chapter) were in action for much of the day. The first call came at noon following a report of two people in the water on the Sefton shoreline. *Hurley Spirit* (H-005) was launched and *Charles Dibdin* (B-837), which was launching on exercise, was sent as well. While on the way to the Sefton area, the Atlantic was diverted back to New Brighton beach to assist a person who was reported to be unconscious, and then returned to Sefton, where the hovercraft had already arrived.

Senior Commander Graham Lowe in charge of the hovercraft reported 'When we arrived in the area north of the river Alt we found two people fishing purposely up to their waists in water and not in any difficulty. We advised them if they intended to fish like this in the future to please contact HM Coastguard with details of when, where and how long as its very easy for well intentioned

Above: Charles Dibdin (Civil Service No.51) (B-837) leaves the boathouse on King's Parade on exercise, March 2014. This house has accommodated three generations of Atlantic rigid-inflatable ILB.

Left and below: Charles Dibdin (Civil Service No.51) (B-837) launching on exercise. (Nicholas Leach)

Charles Dibdin (Civil Service No.51) (B-837) on exercise in the Mersey on a blustery spring day in March 2014. (Nicholas Leach)

members of the public to misunderstand and call for help.'

Just as the hovercraft was returning to station, a further request for assistance was received with a person stuck in mud on Crosby shore. The hovercraft was launched and the lifeboat was asked to go to the area and stand by. Fortunately it was low water so no one was in immediate danger of drowning. A female was found, about 500m north of Crosby baths, stuck in mud up to her thighs and the hovercraft crew were able to pull her out and take her to a waiting Coastguard team. Then they were called to help a male, female and child in soft mud but not actually stuck, and lifted them to safety. Graham Lowe said afterwards: 'We cannot stress enough the need to check out and observe warning signs on the beach at Crosby.'

In 2014 the relief Atlantic 85 *John and Louisa Fisher* (B-870) was on duty, and on Sunday 27 July 2014 she had a busy day as a variety calls were made on the New Brighton's volunteers. Thousands of people had come to Liverpool and the Wirral to watch the visiting tall ships sail away at noon at the end of their visit to the city. In New Brighton the Wallasey Model Boat Society were holding their annual fund-raising day on behalf of the lifeboat station. The day started when the relief Atlantic 85 and crew scattered ashes

Above and left: Charles Dibdin (Civil Service No.51) (B-837) on a routine exercise in the Mersey, March 2014. (Nicholas Leach)

Below: Atlantic 85 Charles Dibdin (Civil Service No.51) (B-837) in the Mersey, March 2014. (Nicholas Leach)

Atlantic 85 Charles Dibdin
(Civil Service No.51) (B-837)
and hovercraft Hurley
Spirit (H-005) together in
the Mersey, August 2014.
(Bob Warwick)

Atlantic 85 Charles Dibdin
(Civil Service No.51) (B-837)
on exercise in the Mersey,
August 2014. (Bob Warwick)

off the sea wall at New Brighton, followed by providing part of
the safety net in the Mersey for the tall ships' departure. After the
ashes had been scattered, the lifeboat arrived off the Pier Head at
Liverpool where hundreds of people lined the sea wall.

At 12.30pm a vessel got into difficulty in a hazardous situation
off the embankment in Leasowe Bay. Although the seas was fairly
calm in the shelter of the river, choppy seas were encountered
once out of the river as the Atlantic went to Leasowe Bay while
an overheating warning light started showing for the port engine,
which was then running intermittently. The lifeboat found the
7.5m fishing vessel, with a crew of four, had its anchor down but

Atlantic 85 Charles Dibdin (Civil Service No.51) (B-837) on service on 22 July 2013 assisting a 60ft yacht with a crew of three which had become grounded on the groyne off near New Brighton lighthouse. The yacht was towed off at high water and towed to Langton Dock. (Bob Warwick)

with engine failure, and it was almost on the embankment wall not far from Leasowe lighthouse. The tide was just turning and the vessel in very shallow water and likely to go aground.

The lifeboat could not get close without damage, but fortunately one of our Wirral's beach lifeguards' jet-skis was also on scene, and they were able to get a line onto the vessel. The anchor rope was cut and, although one of the Atlantic's engines was overheating, the lifeboat crew had to risk it and used both engines to tow the vessel into deeper water and to safety. In view of the sea conditions, the weight of the craft and that only one engine was working reliably, Hoylake lifeboat *Lady of Hilbre* was tasked to take the vessel in tow

Lifeboat crew gather for the Remembrance Day parade on 9 November 2014. (Bob Warwick)

Above: Relief Atlantic 85 John and Louisa Fisher (B-870) launching on exercise. The lifeboat was funded from the legacy of Marion English, of Worsley, Greater Manchester, and named in memory of her parents. She was formally christened on 30 May 2014 at the RNLI College in Poole, and her first relief duty was at New Brighton. (Nicholas Leach)

Right: Relief Atlantic 85 John and Louisa Fisher (B-870) on exercise, November 2014. Construction work on the Port of Liverpool's new deepwater container terminal is evident in the background. (Nicholas Leach)

to a suitable mooring at Tranmere. When *Lady of Hilbre* arrived, the Hoylake crew took over the tow.

While at the show, the crew met a dalek who was asking for donations to the RNLI as an alternative to being exterminated, which, though somewhat out of character, was appreciated nonetheless. The models on display and in action on the lake ranged from a selection of lifeboats to classic Mersey Ferries. With raffles, sales and plenty more £700 was raised by the modellers.

At the end of the day two further incidents occurred in which the lifeboat was involved: the first came after tractor driver Mike Jones raised the alarm at 6.30pm when he saw a small fishing vessel in difficulty, with three people on board, about 700m from Marine Point. The vessel's main and auxiliary engines had both failed and

so the craft was recovered at Victoria slipway. Meanwhile, another fishing vessel had suffered engine failure, and this craft and its crew of three were located mid-river off the slipway and assisted ashore.

On 21 November 2014 John and Louisa Fisher (B-870) was involved in a challenging service, launching during the evening to a 27ft yacht, with a crew of two, which was aground off the Queens Channel on the approach to the Mersey. The lifeboat put out at 5.50pm on what was a cold and dark evening, with conditions offshore difficult and heavy rain making for very poor visibility, compounded by a large and choppy swell, and force five to six winds. Southport's independent lifeboat had also been launched. The New Brighton crew eventually found the yacht, which had managed to get afloat on the incoming tide, in a dangerous position near the Training Wall at the edge of the Queens Channel, just off the busy sea lane. Lifeboat crew Stu Ward was placed on board the yacht to assist with the journey to Liverpool Marina.

Relief Atlantic 85 B-870 arrived on 14 June 2014, when B-837 was taken to the RNLI Inshore Lifeboat Centre at Cowes for her first major refit, which also involved an upgrade to the Sims navigation system and the electronics. (Nicholas Leach)

New Brighton lifeboat crew wearing the latest design of life-jacket. (Nicholas Leach)

The yacht crew of two had taken a battering from the weather on their journey south, and fortunately the yacht did not appear damaged. The two lifeboats escorted the yacht to Liverpool Marina. New Brighton's Lifeboat Operations Manager Graham Sale commented afterwards: 'It was a difficult night for our crew, weather conditions were foul and it was a long cold job. Dedication and training made it possible to return safely.'

Flying to the Rescue

New Brighton station had been operating an inshore lifeboat for more than three decades when it was chosen to be one of the stations at the forefront of the RNLI's latest innovation – the hovercraft. The RNLI saw the hovercraft as a search and rescue tool with many potential benefits. Coastal areas where tidal marshes and mudflats were a potential hazard, such as the Mersey estuary, were difficult to reach using conventional ILBs, and the hovercraft was seen as a way to cover such areas and reach people should they get into difficulty there. As mud rescues could be dangerous and slow to execute using boats, a hovercraft, which could reach a casualty in such circumstances quickly and effect a rescue much more safely, brought a new dimension to the capabilities of lifeboat stations.

The RNLI began assessing the potential of hovercraft in 2001. During the assessment, it was specified that the hovercraft must operate safely in different terrains and volunteer crews had to be

Hovercraft Hurley Spirit (H-005) on the beach by Perch Rock lighthouse in October 2004 when she was presented to the media. (Nicholas Leach)

Hovercraft Hurley Spirit (H-005) being launched onto the beach from the trolley towed by Land Rover, and (right) flying across the beach, October 2004. (Nicholas Leach)

able to master 'flying' it. Commercially available craft were trialled and a design by Griffon Hovercraft of Southampton was chosen. A standard 7.6m Griffon 470TD, powered by two propeller-fans over the stern driven by twin 85hp 1.9-litre Volkswagen intercooled and turbocharged electronically-managed diesel engines, was deemed to be the most suitable craft.

The Griffon 470TD, capable of speeds in excess of thirty knots, could seat between six and eight people, including the pilot, or carry a total payload of 470kgs (1,036lbs). It was highly manoeuvrable and capable of operating over land, shallow water, sand banks and mud flats. Conceived specifically for the RNLI as a search and rescue craft, where manoeuvrability in small, remote shallow waters was paramount, the 470TD could return to station on only one engine if necessary. Hovercraft project managers Hugh Fogarty and Tony Stankus described the trials:

'During the evaluation in Poole, we tested a standard Griffon 450TD hovercraft and tried to establish what terrains and conditions it could work with and how much training would be involved for the volunteers who would operate it. The hovercraft

The donor of the hovercraft Hurley Spirit (H-005), Mrs Kay Hurley MBE, on board the craft for the first time, October 2004. (Nicholas Leach)

showed that it could withstand damage, was easy to prepare for launch, worked well over sand and mud, and the crew training was comparable to that undertaken by inshore lifeboat crews. The limitations included its carrying capacity, a maximum of 450kg, an inability to work on porous surfaces and a weather restriction to a wind speed of less than twenty-five knots and wave height of less than 0.6m (2ft).'

Following the trials at Poole, and as part of the hovercraft pilot scheme, the craft was taken to five lifeboat stations that had been involved in incidents in which a hovercraft might have been of use and because extensive sand or mud flats in the stations' areas of operation were difficult for existing lifeboats to cover. Morecambe, Hunstanton Flint and West Kirby, and Southend-on-Sea were the chosen stations. Two weeks of trials were undertaken at each station, while experienced volunteer lifeboat crew members involved in the testing made comments which helped the project team decide that hovercraft could have a practical use for search and rescue.

Morecambe became the first station to be sent a hovercraft when, in December 2002, *The Hurley Flyer* (H-002) was declared operational. The RNLI had already ordered three further hovercraft from Griffon by then, and the first of these was sent to Hunstanton, the next to Southend-on-Sea and the last to New Brighton, which was deemed to be a better place to locate the hovercraft than West Kirby or Flint. On 23 December 2003 the RNLI announced plans to trial the hovercraft at New Brighton, and the craft arrived on 10 February 2004 to begin a rigorous testing programme to determine its suitability for use in the Mersey Estuary, the Dee Estuary, and the sand flats around the Wirral. The RNLI's hovercraft operations manager, Tony Stankus, said of the new initiative:

'The aim is to establish whether there is a need for a hovercraft in the Wirral area. We have chosen New Brighton as the venue for these trials because it gives us good access to many areas on that stretch of coastline. At the moment we can't say for certain if the hovercraft will be based there permanently, though the trials will give us a good indication of suitability for the area.'

The craft was tested on the Mersey, taken along the beach at Southport, and visited the Coastguard station at Crosby. It was taken as far as possible up the Mersey, going down to Warrington Wier, twenty miles from New Brighton, and under Runcorn Bridge. It also went up the river Dee, and was taken to the North Wales coast as far as Talacre. The purpose-built launching trailer was also driven around the Wirral peninsula to determine the best access points to mud flats and beaches. The extensive trials proved that New Brighton was a suitable place from which to operate a hovercraft, so H-005 was allocated to the station and in June 2004 ten crew attended a hovercraft training course in Poole.

The craft built for New Brighton, H-005, arrived at the station in October 2004, and was officially launched on 29 October 2004 with local supporters, press and media representatives witnessing

Hovercraft Hurley Spirit (H-005) with relief Atlantic 75 Walters Lifeboat (B-723) in the river Mersey, October 2004. (Nicholas Leach)

the event. The £135,000 craft was donated by Mrs Kay Hurley MBE, who had also funded the Morecambe hovercraft, and Mrs Hurley was present to see the new craft being put through its paces on the sandbanks at the mouth of the river Mersey on that grey October day. The relief Atlantic 75 *Walters Lifeboat* (B-723) was also launched and accompanied the hovercraft. The new craft was kept in a facility some distance from the ILB station, and the crew completed several months of intensive training to enable them to effectively fly the hovercraft and operate the special launch rig.

H-005 was formally named *Hurley Spirit* on 25 June 2005 during a ceremony at West Cheshire Sailing Club, on Harrison Drive, at the west end of the Promenade. Although the hovercraft had been sent to the station in October 2004, it was only officially placed on service two days before the ceremony, at which point it was moved into the purpose-built house adjacent to the Sailing Club near where the naming ceremony was held. The station was then operating from two sites, at opposite ends of New Brighton promenade, although the long-term plan was to have a new lifeboat station to house both Atlantic ILB and hovercraft.

The naming ceremony, attended by a many well-wishers and supporters of the station, was chaired by Frank Brereton, Chairman of the station, with the donor, Mrs Kay Hurley MBE, handing over the hovercraft and talking about her admiration for the volunteer lifeboat crews. After the service of dedication led by the Rev Canon Frank Caine, the hovercraft was named by Mrs Hurley, who poured champagne over the craft, which was then taken for a short demonstration across the sands and into the water.

The craft was initially moved by road using a trailer towed by a Land Rover, but a purpose-built rig was subsequently sent to

Hovercraft Hurley Spirit (H-005) leaving the water and going onto the beach, October 2004. (Nicholas Leach)

Above: The naming ceremony of hovercraft Hurley Spirit (H-005) on 25 June 2005, with donor Mrs Hurley christening the craft with champagne before (left) going for a trip across the sands on the craft.

Below: Hovercraft Hurley Spirit (H-005) on the road-going trailer, pulled by Land Rover, used to take her to suitable launch sites. (Photos by Nicholas Leach)

the station which enabled the craft and her crew to be safely and quickly moved around the Wirral to different launch sites as necessary, depending on the location of a casualty. And since going on station, the hovercraft has performed many rescues, fulfilling the role for which it was intended by assisting people stuck in inaccessible places. Typical of the rescues it has been involved in was one which took place on the afternoon of 31 January 2011, when H-005 *Hurley Spirit* was called out to help a man stuck in

Station personnel and volunteer crew after the naming of hovercraft Hurley Spirit (H-005) on 25 June 2005. (Nicholas Leach)

Hovercraft Hurley Spirit (H-005) on the snads at the western end of the Promenade, with the historic Leosowe lighthouse in the background. (Nicholas Leach)

the mud off Egremont promenade at the bottom of Maddock Road, Wallasey. The man, aged thirty-five, was up to his waist in the sticky mud and was fortunate to be seen by a group of teenagers, who promptly called the Coastguard. The weather was bright and sunny though cold, and the tide was nearing low water when the hovercraft was called out. The hovercraft was ideal for crossing on the mud the reach the casualty, as volunteer Hovercraft Commander, Graham Lowe, explained:

'Over the years we have had many call outs for people stuck in this area – the mud is particularly treacherous and people need to take notice of the warning signs. In this case we arrived just as a Fire Service team member had reached him with a rescue board that enabled him to push down onto it and escape the grip of

The Iveco crew cab HT02 vehicle, which was converted to carry the hovercraft, is brought out of the house at the western end of the Promenade with the hovercraft mounted on the flat bed. (Nicholas Leach)

The Iveco crew cab with hovercraft H-005 outside the house at the western end of the Promenade, which has been used since the hovercraft arrived in 2005. (Nicholas Leach)

the mud. We promptly got him on board the hovercraft, wrapped him in a blanket and returned to New Brighton. He was cold and his right leg had gone numb – an ambulance was called and he was taken to hospital for a check up.' The rescued man was a regular walker in the area and had never had any difficulty there, admitting later he was 'very embarrassed but really appreciative of the help he had received'.

Another mud rescue took place on 27 July 2014. At 4pm the station was advised that a person was stuck up to the chest in mud on the Crosby shore, so H-005 *Hurley Spirit*, with a crew of four, was launched and quickly crossed the Mersey estuary. On the busy Crosby beach RNLI Lifeguards were keeping people calm, away from the scene, warning of the dangers in the area and directing the hovercraft to the casualty. Meanwhile the HM Coastguard mud rescue teams were preparing to deploy their equipment when the hovercraft arrived. In charge of the hovercraft, Senior Commander Graham Lowe described what happened next:

'We found the casualty was about half a mile out from the Crosby beach, halfway along and about 10m out from the sewer outlet

Exercise launch of hovercraft
H-005 on the beach by
the Marine Promenade. To
launch, the Iveco's bed is
lowered onto the ground and
the hovercraft can fly off.
(Nicholas Leach)

Below: Hovercraft Hurley
Spirit (H-005) on the beach
with Atlantic 85 Charles
Dibdin (Civil Service No.51)
(B-837) in the Mersey on
exercise. (Nicholas Leach)

pipe, in an area of very soft sand and mud. The casualty, a female, was deeply embedded in the soft mud and had been stuck for about forty minutes. She was very frightened and cold, even though it was one of the hottest days of the summer as the mud just drains away body heat. Our pilot Chris Henderson skilfully brought the hovercraft to within a few inches behind her. Myself and crewman Mike Jones then deployed mud mats around her and these gave us a platform to work from. We reached down into the mud and managed to free her legs and haul a very relieved young lady onto the hovercraft. We wrapped her in a blanket and flew her to the beach and awaiting ambulance and paramedics.'

Commander Lowe added: 'This area of beach has many shifting areas of soft mud and sinking sand which can catch people out. It

The crew on board hovercraft Hurley Spirit (H-005) after a service on 22 June 2014 to people who had got stuck in the mud. It was a busy day for both the hovercraft and Atlantic 85 ILB. Pictured are, left to right, Gary Howland, Chris Henderson (Pilot), Graham Lowe (Senior Commander), Sean Sales and Jim Garland. (Bob Warwick)

Relief Hovercraft Samburgh (H-007) on exercise on the beach with Burbo windfarm. She came on station in September 2014 so that H-005 could be taken to Poole for repairs to the engine. (Nicholas Leach)

Relief Hovercraft Samburgh
(H-007) on exercise
with the station's own
hovercraft Hurley Spirit
(H-005), December 2014.
(Nicholas Leach)

Below: Hurley Spirit (H-005)
being tested after returning
to station in December
2014, on the beach at the
western end of Kings Parade.
(Nicholas Leach)

is vital that attention is paid to the warning signs on the beach and be aware that the tide can come in very quickly. On this occasion it was fortunate that the tide was out, otherwise the outcome may have been tragic.' Also on board the hovercraft during this incident was the RNLI's Divisional Operations Manager Matt Crofts, who was doing a regular inspections of the station, and he commented:

'Having been in RNLI for many years, this was my first opportunity to be a crew member on an actual rescue by hovercraft. I was very impressed with the skill and professionalism shown by Commander Lowe and crew and it clearly demonstrated the effectiveness of the hovercraft to safely get to places otherwise potentially unreachable. The rescue showed the effectiveness of the RNLI lifeboat crews and lifeguards as an integral part of a wider team of emergency agencies. This rescue succeeded because of the smooth inter agency team work between the local HM Coastguard teams, Merseyside Fire & Rescue Service, Ambulance Service and ourselves.'

Having been on station for a decade, hovercraft H-005 *Hurley Spirit* has proved her worth in incidents such as those described above. The craft is now an integral part of the station and has helped to improve rescue coverage in and around the Mersey, showing the benefits of stationing a hovercraft at New Brighton.

Appendices

A • Lifeboat summary

Years on station (launches/saved)	Dimensions Type	Cost ON	Year built Builder	Name Donor
NO.1 STATION				
1.1863 – 12.1876 (40/179)	42' x 10' Tubular	£230 —	1862 Hamilton, Liverpool	*Rescue*/1867- *Willie and Arthur* RNLI Funds/ 1867- Joseph Leather
11.1866 – 8.1867 (1/14)	34'6" x 8' Self-righter	£143.14.8 —	1860 Forrestt, Limehouse	*Latimer* (temporary) Duke of Northumberland
12.1876 – 1888 (22/17)	45' x 11' Tubular	£562 71	1876 Hamilton, Liverpool	*Willie and Arthur* Gift Joseph Leather, Liverpool
1888 – 10.1898 (15/59)	43' x 12'6" Tubular	£637 221	1888 Naval Co, Barrow	*Henry Richardson* Legacy of Mr H.T. Richardson, Bala
10.1898 – 1918 (9/26)	43' x 12'6" Watson	£694 414	1898 Reynolds, Lowestoft	*Henry Richardson* Legacy of Mr H.T. Richardson, Bala
1919 – 12.1930 (7/0)	40' x 11' Watson	£2279.1.4 637	1915 Thames IW/Saunders	*Staughton* Legacy of Miss Mary Staughton, Bedford
11.1930 – 1936 (5/2)	43' x 12'6" Watson	£1759 550	1905 Thames IW, Blackwall	*Anne Miles* Gift Miss Anne Miles, London
1938 – 9.1950 (1923–50: 94/248)	60' x 15' Barnett (M)	£16,084 682	1923 J.S. White, Cowes	*William and Kate Johnston* Gift of Mrs W.H. Kendall and Stewart Johnston, Liverpool; and funds raised by the Liverpool Lifeboat Fund
9.1950 – 4.1973 (215/116)	52' x 13'6" Barnett (M)	£29,264 883	1950 J.S. White, Cowes	*Norman B. Corlett* Gift of Mr W.E. Corlett and his family
NO.2 STATION				
7.1864-4.67 (9/5)	33' x 8'2" Self-righter	£351 —	1863 Hepworth, Millwall	*Willie and Arthur* Gift of Joseph Leather, Liverpool
4.1867-10.78 (4/0)	32' x 7'6" Self-righter	£247.15.0 —	1867 Woolfe, Shadwell	*Lily* Gift Mr Joseph Leather, Liverpool
10.1878-8.88 (9/47)	40' x 8'10" Tubular	£500 —	1878 Hamilton, Liverpool	*Stuart Hay* Gift John Hay & Co, Liverpool
5.1893-10.97 (29/14)	50' x 14'3" Steam	£5,000 231	1889 Green, Blackwall	*Duke of Northumberland* RNLI Funds
27.10.1897-9.1923 (81/196)	55' x 16'6" Steam	£5,145 404	1897 Thornycroft, Chiswick	*Queen* RNLI Funds
13.8.1923-1938 (1923-50: 94/248)	60' x 15' Barnett (M)	£16,084 682	1923 J.S. White, Cowes	*William and Kate Johnston* Gift of Mrs W.H. Kendall and Stewart Johnston, Liverpool; and funds raised by the Liverpool Lifeboat Fund

(M) denotes motor lifeboat

Years on station (launches/saved)	Dimensions Type	Cost ON	Year built Builder	Name Donor
12.1938 – 9.1950 (69/80)	41' x 11'8" Watson (M)	£6,533.10.2 812	1938 Grives & Guttridge	*Edmund and Mary Robinson* Gift of Mrs Mary Robinson, Liverpool
1936 – 1938 (0/0)	43' x 12'6" Watson	£1,694 535	1904 Thames IW, Blackwall	*Charlie Medland* Gift of Charles Medland, Clapham
NO.3 STATION				
7.1884 – 2.1987 (0/0)	46'2" x 11'1" Self-righter	£583.10.0 76	1884 Woolfe, Shadwell	*(Not named)* RNLI Funds

Inshore lifeboats and hovercraft

Years on station	Dimensions Type	ON	Name (if any) Donor
5–8.1973	15'6" x 6'4" D class inflatable	D-42	— —
3.1973 – 3.1981	22'9" x 7'6" Atlantic 21	B-509	— Gift of Mrs F. M. Walker, in memory of her father, mother and brother
4.3.1981 – 1.1996	22'9" x 7'6" Atlantic 21	B-549	*Blenwatch* Fred. Olsen Line
1.1996 – 11.2009	24' x 8'8" Atlantic 75	B-721	*Rock Light* Appeal by the Port and City of Liverpool Branch of RNLI
11.11.2009 –	8.3m x 2.9m Atlantic 75	B-837	*Charles Dibdin (Civil Service No.51)* The Lifeboat Fund
10.2004 –	7.6m x 2.55m Hovercraft	H-005	*Hurley Spirit* Gift of Mrs Kay Hurley MBE, Oxfordshire

Atlantic 85 Charles Dibdin (Civil Service No.51) (B-837) was placed on station in November 2009. (Nicholas Leach)

B • Lifeboat details

Rescue/Willie and Arthur

On station	No.1 station 1863 – 1876
Record	40 launches, 179 lives saved
Dimensions	42ft x 10ft x 4ft
Type	Tubular, 14-oared
Cost	£230
Donor	RNLI Funds, 1867 appropriated to the gift of Jospeh Leather, Liverpool
Built	1862, Hamilton, Garston, Liverpool
Notes	Driven ashore and damaged, 30.1.1877

Willie and Arthur

On station	No.2 station 7.1864 – 3.1867
Record	9 launches, 5 lives saved
Dimensions	33ft x 8ft 2in x 3ft 10in
Type	Self-righter, 10-oared, iron hulled
Cost	£351
Donor	Gift of Mr J. Leather, Liverpool
Built	1863, Hepworth, Millwall
Notes	Built for Teignmouth, named China, designed by Joseph Prowse; sold 1874

Latimer

On station	No.1 station 1866 – 1867
Record	1 launches, 14 lives saved
Dimensions	34ft 6in x 8ft x 3ft 6in
Type	Peak self-righter, 12-oared
Cost	£143 14s 8d
Donor	Duke of Northumberland
Built	1860, Forrest, Limehouse

Lily

On station	No.2 station 1867 – 1878
Record	4 launches, 0 lives saved
Dimensions	32ft x 7ft 6in
Type	Self-righter, 10-oared
Cost	£247 15s 0d
Donor	Gift Mr Joseph Leather, Liverpool
Built	1867, Woolfe, Shadwell
Notes	Sold 1889

Willie and Arthur

Official Number	71
On station	No.1 station 1876 – 88
Record	22 launches, 17 lives saved
Dimensions	45ft x 11ft
Type	Tubular, 14-oared
Cost	£562
Donor	Gift of Mr Joseph Leather, Liverpool
Built	1876, Hamilton, Garston, Liverpool
Notes	Worn out and sold for scrap, 4.1890

Stuart Hay

On station	No.2 station 10.1878 – 8.88
Record	9 launches, 47 lives saved
Dimensions	40ft x 8ft 10in
Type	Tubular, 12-oared
Cost	£500
Donor	Gift from John Hay & Co, Liverpool
Built	1878, Hamilton, Garston, Liverpool
Notes	Sold and broken up 1898

Un-named

Official Number	76
On station	No.3 station 7.1884 – 2.1887
Record	0 launches, 0 lives saved
Dimensions	46ft 2in x 11ft 1in
Type	Self-righter, 12-oared
Cost	£583 10d 0d
Donor	Gift of Mrs G Carew.
Built	1884, Woolfe, Shadwell
Notes	Originally named *Edith*; sold 1894

Henry Richardson

Official Number	221
On station	28.8.1888 – 10.98, No.2 1888-92, No.1 1892-98
Record	15 launches, 59 lives saved
Dimensions	43ft x 12ft 6in
Type	Tubular, 14-oared
Cost	£637
Weight	7 tons
Donor	Legacy of Mr Henry T. Richardson, Bala, Wale
Built	1888, Naval Construction and Armaments Co, Barrow-in-Furness
Notes	Took part in the Lowestoft sailing trials in 1892; went via the Forth and Clyde Canal to Lowestoft to be compared with other types of lifeboat; a 46ft Norfolk and Suffolk, 44ft self-righter and 43ft Watson; broken up 1898

Duke of Northumberland

Official Number	231
On station	17 May 1893 – October 1997
Record	29 launches, 14 lives saved
Dimensions	50ft x 14ft 3in x 5ft 9in
Type	Steam
Cost	£5,000
Weight	24 tons
Donor	RNLI Funds
Built	1889, R. & H. Green, Blackwall
Notes	Hull divided into 15 watertight compts; driven by water jets, engine by Thorneycroft, of Chiswick, with cylinders 18.5in and 14.5in, and a stroke of 12in, developing 170hp; sold 1923

Queen

Official Number	404
On station	27 October 1897 – 13 August 1923
Record	81 launches, 196 lives saved

Dimensions	55ft x 16ft 6in x 5ft 6in
Type	Steam
Cost	£5,145
Weight	31 tons 18 cwt
Donor	RNLI Funds
Built	1897, Thornycroft, Chiswick
Notes	Driven by water jets, compound engine by builders, fired by a Thorneycroft patent water-tube boiler working at a pressure of 145lbs; turbine propelled, single 198hp compound engine driven by water jets, eight relieving tubes
Disposal	Sold 1924 at auction for £75 to Captain J.D.H. Filbee for pleasure trips at New Brighton, but permission was refused so she was sold again in 1925; Elder Dempster shippnig line bought her and shipped her to Sekondi, West Africa and, after alterations had been carried out, she was used for carrying passengers to the shore at surf ports.

Henry Richardson

Official Number	414
On station	October 1898 – October 1919
Record	9 launches, 26 lives saved
Dimensions	43ft x 12ft 6in
Type	Watson, 10-oared
Cost	£694
Weight	12 tons 12 cwt
Donor	Legacy of Mr Henry T. Richardson, Pwllheli
Built	1898, Reynolds, Lowestoft
Notes	Condemned and sold 1919

Staughton

Official Number	637
On station	No.1 station 1919 – December 1930
Record	7 launches, 0 lives saved
Dimensions	40ft x 11ft x 5ft 4in
Type	Watson, 12-oared
Cost	£2,279 1s 4d
Weight	9 tons 9 cwt
Donor	Legacy of Miss Mary Staughton, Bedford
Built	1915, Thames Iron Works, Blackwall; completed by Saunders, Cowes
Notes	Originally ordered in 1912 for Rosslare Harbour but never sent as the station was to be closed.
Disposal	Sold 20.1.1931 for £50 to Henry Hornby & Co, Wallasey, Cheshire

William and Kate Johnston

Official Number	682
On station	13 August 1923 – September 1950
Record	94 launches, 248 lives saved
Dimensions	60ft x 15ft x 7ft 2in
Type	Barnett
Cost	£16,084 8s 10d
Weight	41 tons 5 cwt
Donor	Gifts from Mrs W.H. Kendall and Mr Stewart Johnston, Liverpool; plus money from the Liverpool Motor Lifeboat Fund
Built	1923, J.S. White, Cowes
Notes	Named.24.9.1924 at New Brighton by wife of Stewart Johnston
Disposal	Sold 12.12.1950 for £525 to J. Turner, London

Anne Miles

Official Number	550
On station	No.1 station 16 November 1930 − 1936
Record	5 launches, 2 lives saved
Dimensions	43ft x 12ft 6in x 5ft 11in
Type	Watson, 10-oared
Cost	£1759
Weight	11 tons 15 cwt
Donor	Gift Miss A. Miles, West Hampstead, London
Built	1905, Thames Iron Works, Blackwall
Disposal	Sold 10.10.1936 to Ralph Bonner Pink, Southsea

Charlie Medland

Official Number	535
On station	No.2 station 1936 − 1938
Record	0 launches, 0 lives saved
Dimensions	43ft x 12ft 6in
Type	Watson, 10-oared
Cost	£1,693 13s 4d
Weight	11 tons 13 cwt
Donor	Legacy of Mr Charles Medland, Clapham
Built	1904, Thames Iron Works, Blackwall
Disposal	Sold 8.1.1939 to H.Y.C. Henry, Rochester

Edmund and Mary Robinson

Official Number	812
On station	No.2 station December 1938 − September 1950
Record	69 launches, 80 lives saved
Dimensions	41ft x 11ft 8in
Type	Watson (M)
Cost	£6,533 10s 2d
Weight	14 tons 3 cwt
Donor	Gift of Mrs Mary Robinson, Liverpool
Built	1938, Groves & Guttridge, Cowes
Notes	Named 4.2.1939 at South West Princes Dock, Liverpool, by Mrs Robinson; placed in the Reserve Fleet in 1950 and served at Lizard, New Brighton, Swanage, Weymouth, Arklow, Fleetwood, Weymouth, Donaghadee, Dun Laoghaire, Moelfre, Sennen Cove and Barry Dock
Disposal	Sold 3.1964 to Henry Bray, Mumbles, Swansea

Norman B Corlett

Official Number	883
On station	No.1 station 9.1950 − 4.73
Record	215 launches, 116 lives saved
Dimensions	52ft x 13ft 6in x 4ft 6in
Type	Barnett (M)
Cost	£29,264 9s 5d
Weight	27 tons 18 cwt
Donor	Gift from W. Ernest Corlett and members of his family in memory of his son, drowned in a yachting accident
Built	1950, J.S. White, East Cowes
Notes	Named 29.3.1951 at Princes Dock, Liverpool, by HRH Duchess of Kent
Disposal	Sold 2.1982 to B. Twomey, Crosshaven, Co Cork

C • Summary of services by lifeboats 1863–1973

Rescue Lifeboat (renamed 1867)

1863 May 11 Brig *Levant*, of Bristol, saved 10
June 27 Schooner *Vigilant*, of Kirkcaldy, saved 6
1864 Feb 1 Ship *Contest*, of Liverpool, saved vessel and 18
Apr 19 Barque *Corea*, of Guernsey, assisted to save vessel and 12
1865 Oct 28 Schooner *Earl of Zetland*, of Amlwch, saved vessel and 5

Willie and Arthur Lifeboat (formerly *Rescue*)

1867 Dec 6 Ship *Thornton*, of New York, saved 13
1868 Nov 3 Ship *Grand Bonny*, of Liverpool, stood by
1869 Sep 26 Barque *Empress*, of Prince Edward Island, saved 18
Oct 19 Schooner *Elephant*, of Ulverston, saved 1
1870 Apr 2 Lifeboat *Lily*, of New Brighton (No.2), rendered assistance
May 12 Barque *Ida Maria*, of Danzig, saved 14
Aug 29 Flat *Rattler*, of Liverpool, saved 5
Sep 17 Schooner *Gomez de Castro*, stood by
1872 Apr 22 Brigantine *Thomas*, of Dumfries, landed 3 from a pilot boat
Nov 16 Barque *Vale of Nith*, of Liverpool, assisted to save vessel and 21
1873 Aug 10 Ship *Dunmail*, of Liverpool, saved 10
1875 Sep 27 Ship *Ellen Southerd*, of Richmond (Maine), saved 8
Liverpool tubular lifeboat, saved 11
1876 Jan 17 Barque *Brother's Pride*, of St John's, saved 11
Mar 4 Schooner *Iona*, of Belfast, saved 3

Willie and Arthur (second) Lifeboat

1877 Jan 28 Sloop *Darling*, of Beaumaris, saved vessel and 2
30 Barque *John E. Chase*, of Savannah, stood by
Feb 20 Italian barque, rendered assistance
Ship *Marietta*, of Liverpool, saved 13
Nov 23 Steamer *Bohemian*, of Liverpool, stood by
1881 Jan 4 Steamship *Brazilian*, of Barrow, rendered assistance
1885 Jan 11 Steamship *Venetian*, of Liverpool, stood by
Dec 3 Schooner *Nathaniel*, of Aberystwyth, assisted to save vessel

Henry Richardson (second) Lifeboat

1902 Oct 15 Steamship *Heraclides*, of Liverpool, saved boat and 22
1918 June 15 Motor ketch *E.D.J.*, of Newcastle, saved 4

Staughton Lifeboat

1925 July 17 Yacht *Lady Dorothy*, of New Brighton, rendered assistance

Ann Miles Lifeboat

1934 May 5 Boat of steam tug *Yorkgarth*, of Liverpool, saved 2

City of Bradford Relief Lifeboat

1938 June 10 Schooner *Minnie*, of Peterhead, saved vessel and 4

William and Kate Johnston Lifeboat

Oct 2 Boat *Kestrel*, of Liverpool, saved boat and 2
Nov 23 Fishing boat *Progress*, of Hoylake, saved 3
Schooner *Lochranza Castle*, of Wick, saved 4

1939 Mar 8 Crosby lightvessel, saved 5
Nov 24 Steamship *Regu*, of Glasgow, saved 103
1940 Jan 4 HM Destroyer *Whirlwind*, gave help
Nov 2 Motor vessel *Bolham*, of Chester, landed 4
15 Steamship *Penrhyn*, of Liverpool, landed 5
21 Steamship *Nord Est II*, of Belfast, stood by
Dec 27 Steamship *Lady Connaught*, of Dublin, escorted
1941 Mar 13 Steamship *Ullapool*, of West Hartlepool, landed 14
1942 Jan 12 Fishing boat *Never Mind*, of Liverpool, saved boat and 2
1943 June 3 Fishing boat *Speedwell*, of New Brighton, escorted
1944 Jan 1 Burbo Bank Military Fort, landed sick man, saving 1
1945 June 9 Naval Cadet motor boat *Freelance*, saved boat
29 HDML 41360, escorted
1947 Sep 22 Queen's Fort, landed 6
1948 Sep 15 Hopper *Tatam II*, of London, landed 8
1949 Aug 7 Converted ship's boat *Margie*, of Wallasey, saved boat and 6
Sep 2 Schooner *Susan Vittery*, of Cork, stood by
5 Fishing boat *Greyhound*, gave help
16 Yacht *Blue Waters*, saved yacht and 2

Norman B. Corlett Lifeboat

1951 Feb 10 Punt, gave help
Mar 1 Steamship *British Dragoon*, of London, gave help
July 27 Persons cut off by the tide, gave help
Aug 7 Sailing boat *Permit*, saved boat and 3
20 Motor cruisers *Sea Gull* and *Bill*, stood by
25 Yacht *Sirius*, gave help
Oct 22 Motor launch *Vanadia*, of Ayr, escorted
1952 Mar 11 Fishing boat *Speedwell*, of New Brighton, gave help
24 Fishing boat *Emma*, of Rock Ferry, stood by
June 14 Motor boat of HMS *Conway*, gave help
July 7 Sailing dinghy, gave help
20 Motor boat *Adelaide*, of Liverpool, saved boat and 2
Aug 31 Sailing dinghy, landed 1
Oct 6 Steamship *Bannrose*, of Liverpool, escorted
Dec 17 Tanker *Rinda*, of Oslo, gave help
1953 Aug 15 Yacht *Lesley*, saved yacht and 4
Sep 25 Yacht *Minx*, gave help
Oct 18 Motor vessel *Vitesse*, of Delfzijl, stood by
1954 May 5 Five sailing dinghies, landed 7 and gave help
June 13 Yacht *Jean*, saved yacht and 2
July 27 Pontoon, gave help
Aug 1 Yacht *Eilea*, gave help
Nov 21 Dinghy *Horace*, of New Brighton gave help
1955 May 1 Fishing boat *Kitty*, escorted
July 3 Seven yachts, escorted
23 Pinnace *Rosie*, landed 15 and stood by
Pinnace *Black Cap*, stood by
Aug 16 Sailing boat *Genevieve*, gave help
Nov 12 Steamship *Bannprince*, of Liverpool, landed 6
26 Fishing boat *Cresswell*, of Liverpool, gave help and landed 2

1956 Feb 16 Hopper *Mersey No.24*, of Liverpool, saved 5

City of Glasgow Reserve Lifeboat

July 29 Yacht *Troglodyte*, saved yacht and 3
         Yacht *Juliet Bella*, saved 2

Norman B. Corlett Lifeboat

Aug 1 Cabin cruiser *Merry Widow*, gave help
24 Hopper barge *James 96*, of London, escorted
Sep 30 Naval whaler, saved whaler and 4
        Yacht *Gypsy*, saved yacht and 3
Nov 29 Trawler *Burma Emerald*, of London, gave help
1957 Jan 3 Bar Lightvessel, landed a sick man, saving 1
8 Motor vessel *Ousel*, of Liverpool, stood by
26 Motor vessel *Defender*, of Liverpool, stood by
Mar 16 Canoe, saved canoe and 2
Apr 21 Yacht, escorted
May 18 Fishing boat *Mary*, saved 2
26 Naval whaler, gave help
Oct 6 Yacht *Rango*, stood by
Nov 5 Motor vessel *J.B. Kee*, of Castletown, saved 6
1958 Mar 30 Aircraft, gave help
Apr 19 Yacht *Thebe*, gave help
May 7 Rubber dinghy, saved 1
23 Converted ship's boat, saved boat and 5
July 13 Cadet whaler, saved whaler and 7
Aug 31 Fishing boats *Rosebud* and *Marion*, saved boats
        and 9
Sep 3 Two yachts, stood by
Oct 4 Motor vessel *Lecoteau*, gave help
Dec 15 Yacht *Nomad*, gave help and landed 2
1959 Jan 26 Boat in distress, escorted
Apr 23 Sailing boat *Volga*, gave help
July 25 Cabin cruiser *Sea Gull*, gave help

White Star Reserve Lifeboat

No services

Norman B. Corlett Lifeboat

1960 July 18 Motor vessels *Denbigh Coast*, of Liverpool, and
                Irish Maple, of Limerick, gave help
Oct 2 Fishing boat *Sea Fisher*, saved boat and 3
1961 Jan 21 Motor vessels *Lurcher*, in collision with
                Stamatios G. Embiricos, of Andros, landed 12
May 7 Yacht *Rondinella*, saved yacht and 3
June 16 Converted ship's boat *Shandra*, escorted
Sep 16 Motor vessel *Paul Westers*, of Groningen, esc'd
Oct 20 Steamship *Ulefoss*, of Oslo, escorted

White Star Reserve Lifeboat

1961-2 No services

Norman B. Corlett Lifeboat

1962 July 21 Outboard motor dinghy, saved dinghy and 2
29 Canoe, gave help
Aug 5 Yacht *Tricia*, of New Brighton, saved yacht
        and 6
Sep 9 Yacht *Clueless*, saved yacht
23 Yacht, saved a dinghy
1963 Apr 29 Dinghy *Naneia*, saved dinghy and 2

White Star Reserve Lifeboat

June 4 Boys marooned by the tide, saved 4
22 Yacht *Therese*, escorted
    Yacht *Ariel*, saved yacht
    Yacht *Wind Bush*, escorted
July 26 Motor vessel *Cristo*, of Bristol, stood by

Aug 5 Fishing boat *Phoenician*, gave help
16 Catamaran *Spindrift*, saved vessel and 3
24 Bar Lightvessel, landed a body
Oct 18 Fishing boat in tow of another, stood by
Nov 10 Dinghy, saved dinghy and 2
12 Tanker *Helen*, of Stavanger, escorted

J.J.K.S.W. Reserve Lifeboat

1964 Sep 6 Cabin cruiser *Lucelle*, saved boat and 2
Oct 7 Boat of sand dredger *John L.K.*, of Liverpool,
        gave help
Nov 1 Pilot launch, landed a sick man

Norman B. Corlett Lifeboat

1965 Mar 12 Speedboat, gave help
Apr 9 Sailing dinghy, saved dinghy and 2
Aug 1 Fishing boat and rubber dinghy, saved both
        craft and 5
24 RNLB *Oldham IV*, of Hoylake, escorted
Oct 19 Motor vessel *Ballylesson*, of Belfast, stood by
22 Motor vessel *Salaverry*, of Liverpool, stood by
27 Small motor boat, gave help
1966 Apr 3 Motor fishing vessel *Orion*, escorted
June 1 Sailing dinghy and yacht club rescue boat,
        saved boats and 5
July 2 Sailing boat *Conway*, and yacht *Magweener*,
        saved boats and 7
8 Motor vessel *Banner Cliffe*, stood by
15 Fishing boat *Lily*, of Liverpool, gave help
Aug 9 Speedboat, saved boat and 1
    Yacht *Reedbird*, gave help
20 Cabin cruiser *Comet*, gave help
Aug 27 Speedboat *Sea Swallow*, saved boat and 2
Sep 11 Motor boat *Vagois*, in tow of motor boat *Trust*
        in Providence, gave help
Oct 15 Motor fishing boat *Diana*, gave help
Nov 27 Bar Lightvessel, took out a doctor
Dec 3 Bar Lightvessel, landed a sick man
1967 Apr 16 Motor vessel *Middledale H*, of Hull, gave help
June 5 Sailing dinghy, saved dinghy and 2
10 Motor boat *Gem*, gave help and landed 5
Sep 8 Ferry boat *Daffodil II*, of Liverpool, landed 30
        and stood by
Nov 18 Cabin cruisers *Pedro* and *Jolly Roger*, gave help

Mary Stanford Reserve Lifeboat

Dec 8 Motor vessel *Farringay*, of Cardiff, in tow of
        motor vessel *Ben Veg*, escorted
1968 Oct 12 Motor vessel *Unterweser*, of Brake, stood by

Norman B. Corlett Lifeboat

1969 Feb 23 Motor vessel *Balmoral Queen*, stood by
May 25 Yacht club rescue launch, landed a body
June 24 Dredger *Cressington*, of Liverpool and motor
                vessel *Hannes Knuppel*, of Hamburg, in
                collision, gave help
July 18 Motor fishing vessel *Peel Castle*, gave help
Aug 3 Fishing boat *Lily*, gave help
    Yacht *Two's Company*, saved yacht and 2
    Yacht *Martlet*, saved yacht
Sep 21 Cabin cruiser *Lara*, saved cruiser and 2
28 Dinghy, saved dinghy and 3

Crawford and Constance Conybeare Reserve Lifeboat

Oct 18 Trimaran *Devil Woman*, saved craft and 5
        Cabin cruiser, saved vessel and 3

Norman B. Corlett Lifeboat

1970	Jan 29	Motor launch *Jan Pet*, escorted
	May 30	Cabin cruiser *Salazar*, saved vessel and 2
		Yacht *Painted Lady*, stood by
	July 21	Capsized boat, recovered a body
	22	Capsized catamaran, recovered a drift float
	Aug 8	Motor boat, saved boat and 4
	22	Yacht *Kael*, gave help
	Sep 17	Yacht *Hieriver*, landed 4
1971	Jan 9	Light at sea, recovered life-belt marker buoy
	May 9	Cabin cruiser *Grey Otter*, saved cruiser and 9
	14	Yacht *Squirrel*, gave help
	22	Cabin cruiser *Alayne*, stood by
	Aug 10	Cabin cruiser *Stella Maris*, saved cruiser and 2
		Yacht *Etain*, saved 4
	Sep 7	Fishing boat *Marie*, gave help
	Oct 3	Motor launch *Pinnace*, gave help and landed 4
1972	May 7	Fishing boat *Marie*, saved 9
	13	Yacht, saved 2
	June 10	Boys marooned on a beacon, landed 2
1973	Jan 24	Cabin cruiser, saved vessel

No.2 station

Willie and Arthur Lifeboat

| 1864 | July 4 | Brigantine *Richard Cobden*, ? service |

Reserve Lifeboat

| 1867 | Feb 25 | Barque Coquimbo, of Sunderland, saved 15 |

Stuart Hay Lifeboat

1880	Feb 12	Steamship *Anatolian*, of Liverpool, stood by
		and transferred 26 to a tug
1883	Oct 5	Ship *Nuncio*, of Yarmouth (NS), saved 21

Henry Richardson Lifeboat

1890	Jan 14	Schooner *Thomas*, of Amlwch, assisted to save
		vessel
1891	Oct 13	Shrimp boat Spray, of New Brighton, saved 3
		Shrimp boat *Sophia*, of New Brighton, saved 2
	Dec 7	Barque *Hannah Landles*, of Glasgow, saved 25
1892	July 19	Schooner *Renown*, of Wigtown, assisted to
		save vessel
		Ship *Maxwell*, of Liverpool, saved 29

Duke of Northumberland Lifeboat

1894	Jan 27	Schooner *Maria Lamb*, of Barrow, saved (also a
		dog) 6
	Feb 13	Steamship *Lady Louisa*, of Liverpool, assisted
		to save abandoned vessel
	23	Schooner *Caroline*, of Fowey, landed 5 from
		Crosby Lightvessel
	Dec 22	Schooner *Faith*, of Beaumaris, saved 3
1895	Mar 28	Schooner *Holly How*, of Barrow, saved 5
	Apr 11	Barque *South African*, of Belfast, stood by
1896	June 11	Ship *Marechal Suchet*, of London, stood by
	July 29	Steamship *Flying Falcon*, of Liverpool, landed
		76 passengers
	Nov 9	Brigantine *Emma Ives*, of Dublin, stood by
1897	Nov 28	Fishing cutter *Rocklight*, of Liverpool, saved
		drifting boat

Queen Lifeboat

1898	Feb 25	Schooner *Robert and Elizabeth*, of Lancaster,
		saved 4
	Aug 5	Steam flat *Bessie*, of Liverpool, stood by

1899	Jan 2	Steamship *Voltaic*, of Belfast, stood by
	Nov 11	Barque *Falcon*, of Laurvig, saved 9
	Dec 30	Steamship *Highland Laird*, of Liverpool,
		rendered assistance and stood by
		Steamship *Albatross*, stood by
1900	Dec 21	Steamship *Angola*, of Glasgow, stood by
1901	Mar 7	Steamship *Dominion*, of Liverpool, stood by
	Dec 24	Schooner *Lizzie*, of Chester, saved 4
1902	Sep 3	Hopper *No.12*, of Liverpool, stood by
1903	Feb 27	Four-masted barque *Fingal*, of Dublin, saved 32
1904	Dec 10	Steamship *Ulloa*, of Barcelona, landed 2
	11	Steamship *Ulloa*, of Barcelona, saved 10
	13	Hopper barge *Rhinoceros*, of London, saved 6
1905	Jan 12	Ship *Kalliope*, of Hamburg, stood by
	Mar 16	Steamship *Innisfallen*, of Cork, stood by
		Two steam hoppers, of Liverpool, stood by
1906	Aug 12	Training brig *James J. Bibby*, of Liverpool,
		stood by and rendered assistance
1907	Aug 7	Schooner *Problem*, of Chester, saved 3
	Dec 8	Sloop *Pilgrim*, of Cemaes, stood by and
		assisted to save vessel
1908	Apr 3	Schooner *James O'Neil*, of Kinsale, stood by
	June 11	Schooner *William Edwards*, of Liverpool,
		assisted to save vessel and 3
1909	Aug 13	Flat *Bessie*, of Liverpool, saved 2
	Dec 3	Steamship *Bellagio*, of Glasgow, stood by
1910	Aug 27	Dredger *Walter Glynn*, of Liverpool, saved 5
1911	June 22	Schooner *Tankerton Tower*, of Faversham,
		landed 5
1913	June 9	Fishing boat, of Liverpool, saved 3
1920	May 23	Steamship *Kurmark*, of London, landed 9
	Aug 21	Paddle steamship *La Marguerite*, of Liverpool,
		stood by
1921	June 19	Fishing boat *Mona*, saved 2
1923	Oct 12	Motor vessel *Garthavon*, of Bristol, stood by
	Nov 16	Steamship *Ibis*, of Liverpool, saved 7
		Steam tug *Spurn*, of Liverpool, saved 5
	Dec 15	Steamship *Armagh*, of London, assisted to save
		104

William and Kate Johnston Lifeboat

1925	Apr 15	Hopper No.9, of Liverpool, gave help
		Hopper No.9, of Liverpool, saved 9
		Hopper No.9, of Liverpool, stood by
	Sep 26	Motor vessel *Innisinver*, of London, saved 5
1926	May 8	Yacht *Mendosa II*, of New Brighton, saved
		yacht
	Nov 14	Cutter *Rita*, of Liverpool, saved cutter and 5
1927	Jun 26	Formby Lightvessel, stood by
	Nov 30	Steamship *Lochmonar*, of London, rendered
		assistance and transported 74 to tugs
	Dec 7	Steamship *Zealand*, of Liverpool, stood by and
		rendered assistance
		Steamship *Ravens Point*, of Liverpool, stood by
		and rendered assistance
1928	Feb 17	Steamship *Varand*, of London, saved 42
	Oct 19	Small boat *Gem*, saved 3
	Nov 24	Steamship *Emile Delmas*, of La Rochelle, saved
		23
1930	June 7	Motor launch *Scintus*, of Liverpool, rendered
		assistance
	Sep 6	Fishing boat *Aysha*, of Garston, rendered
		assistance
	Nov 16	Schooner *Carmenta*, of Plymouth, stood by
1933	Apr 1	Fishing boat *Eagle*, of Bootle, saved boat and 6

July 9 Fishing boat *Mona*, of Liverpool, saved boat and 6

Aug 6 Fishing boat *Madge*, of Liverpool, saved 2

Fishing boat *Bonny Breeze*, of Liverpool, saved boat and 3

1934 Jan 3 Steamship *Landes*, of Liverpool, landed 1

1935 Jan 25 Pilot vessel *Walter J. Chambers* (No.2), of Liverpool, escorted

July 27 Converted ship's boat *Collingwood*, of Liverpool, saved boat and 5

Oct 19 Steamship *Inga 1*, of Bergen , landed 1

Nov 17 Boat *Pamelia June*, of New Brighton, saved boat and 4

1936 Nov 11 Fishing boat *Ione*, of New Brighton, saved boat and 3

30 Motor barge *T.H. Burton*, of Liverpool, saved 4

Edmund and Mary Robinson Lifeboat

1939 June 11 Motor boat *Sally*, of Birkenhead, saved boat and 3

Nov 5 Fishing boat *Queen*, of Liverpool, saved boat and 6

1940 July 23 Fishing boat *Alice*, of New Brighton, escorted

29 Steamship *Ousebridge*, of West Hartlepool, gave help

Liverpool pilot boat, gave help

Oct 5 Steamship *Aquilla*, of Liverpool, escorted

Dec 6 Steamship *Governor*, of Liverpool, escorted

8 Formby Lightvessel, saved 6

1941 May 13 Egremont Landing Stage, gave help

1942 Mar 3 RAF Launch, saved launch and 7

1943 Nov 2 Steamship *Olev*, of Belfast, stood by

Dec 30 Sailing dinghy L.2156, of Wallasey, saved boat and 1

1944 Feb 14 Steamship *Sharpsburg*, of Philadelphia, stood by

Dec 13 Walrus seaplane, saved seaplane and 1

28 Steamship *Wallasey*, of Wallasey, landed 102

1945 Mar 29 Fishing boat *Agnes*, of Preston, saved 3

1946 May 1 Rowing boat *Dot*, saved boat and 2

June 5 Motor yacht *Gannet*, of Glasgow, saved yacht and 3

10 Yachts *Puffin*, *Sheila*, *Iduna* and *Pastime*, of Egremont, escorted

July 14 Yacht *Viola*, saved yacht

18 Steamship *Denham*, of Liverpool, landed an injured man

19 Fishing boat *Greyhound*, of Liverpool, saved boat and 1

22 A float, of Rhyl, salved float

23 A float, of Rhyl, salved float

1947 Jan 13 Motor fishing boat *Lilian*, of Fleetwood, escorted

Nov 15 Bar Lightvessel, landed an injured man

1948 Jan 18 Motor vessel *Guloy*, of Bergen, rendered assistance

26 Fishing vessel *Moa*, saved 3

28 RASC Tender *Sir Herbert Miles*, saved 25

Small boat, saved 9

Feb 21 Queens Forts works, landed a sick man and another man

May 7 Queens Forts works, landed an injured man

June 9 Fishing boat *Jill*, of Liverpool, gave help

Aug 2 Fishing boat *Ranger*, of Liverpool, saved 4

1950 July 23 Yacht *Jupiter*, of West Kirby, landed 2

Sep 16 Schooner *Happy Harry*, of Arklow, saved 4

Boarding Boat Rescues

This is incomplete as they are only spasmodically recorded in the official service lists.

1896 July 26 Cutter *Gladdies*, of Liverpool, saved 4

1898 Apr 6 Smack *Frederica*, of Liverpool, stood by

1899 Nov 23 Steamship *Coniston Fell*, of Liverpool, transferred 3 to a tug

1902 Mar 25 Fishing boat *Ellen*, of Liverpool, stood by

28 Cutter yacht *Mosquito*, rendered assistance

1920 May 22 Yacht, of Birkenhead, landed 4

1921 June 19 Fishing boat *Mona*, saved 2

1926 Nov 18 Dinghy, saved dinghy and 2

1928 Apr 9 Small boat, saved boat and 2

Sep 19 Small boat, saved boat and 2

30 Two boats, saved boats and 3

1929 Nov 11 Fishing boat *Golden Arrow*, saved boat and 2

1930 June 9 Motor boat *Cintilla*, rendered assistance

Fishing smack *Tern*, of Warrington, stood by

July 21 Motor launch *Cintilla*, landed 1

? Yacht *Mascot*, of New Brighton, saved yacht

1931 Aug 25 Steamship *St Mungo*, of Dublin, landed 2 injured men

1940 Nov 23 Steamship *Bafra*, towed a ship's boat to steamship and landed unconscious man

1941 Sep 28 Small boat, of Egremont, towed in boat and 2 boys

1942 June 7 Landed 25 children from a sand-bank

1943 Aug 20 Brought in an unconscious woman

1944 May 15 US Ambulances stuck in the mud, saved 3

1945 Jan 1 Woman cut off by the tide, saved 1

Feb 18 Army raft, saved raft and 8

Apr 2 Egremont Landing Stage, saved two boys from the girders

June 9 Sea Cadet boat *Freelance*, landed 9

Oct 23 Canvas dinghy, saved dinghy and 1

1946 Apr 12 Canvas dinghy, saved dinghy and 1

Boat of a hopper, saved boat and 5

June 30 People cut off by the tide, saved 4

Aug 13 Boat of yacht *Arabis*, saved boat and 2

Oct 15 Motor launch, saved launch and 1

D • Summary of inshore lifeboat services

Year	ILB	Launches	Saved	Total launches	Total saved
1973	B-509	6	0	11	6
	D-42	3	6		
	ON.883	2	0		
1974	B-500	11	2	32	12
	B-509	16	10		
	D-42	5	0		
1975	B-500	10	3	24	10
	B-509	14	7		
1976	B-509	22	6	22	6
1977	B-509	15	9	15	9
1978	B-509	9	0	13	2
	B-525	4	2		
1979	B-509	15	3	15	3
1980	B-509	33	12	33	12
1981	B-509	4	2	15	10
	B-549	11	8		
1982	B-549	19	7	19	7
1983	B-549	15	0	15	0
1984	B-525	3	2	35	15
	B-549	32	13		
1985	B-525	8	4	16	7
	B-549	8	3		
1986	B-549	13	0	13	0
1987	B-549	26	11	26	11
1988	B-549	27	4	27	4
1989	B-533	7	0	23	5
	B-549	16	5		
1990	B-533	1	0	27	7
	B-549	26	7		
1991	B-549	23	8	23	8
1992	B-549	49	1	49	1
1993	B-549	50	8	50	8
1994	B-549	17	7	43	13
	B-592	26	6		
1995	B-533	15	0	54	4
	B-548	2	0		
	B-549	37	4		
1996	B-709	5	0	39	3
	B-721	34	3		

Year	ILB	Launches	Saved	Total launches	Total saved
1997	B-721	45	11	45	11
1998	B-721	45	4	45	4
1999	B-721	18	8	42	10
	B-723	24	2		
2000	B-721	44	1	44	1
2001	B-721	37	8	37	8
2002	B-721	32	1	32	1
2003	B-721	44	0	44	0
2004	B-721	22	3	37	5
	B-723	10	2		
	B-753	4	0		
	H-005	1	0		
2005	B-721	32	0	41	0
	H-005	9	0		
2006	B-721	55	5	66	5
	H-005	11	0		
2007	B-721	44	2	61	3
	B-723	3	0		
	B-755	4	0		
	H-001	1	0		
	H-005	9	1		
2008	B-721	36	2	45	3
	H-005	9	1		
2009	B-721	30	5	41	5
	B-837	1	0		
	H-005	10	0		
2010	B-837	25	0	34	0
	H-005	6	0		
	H-006	3	0		
2011	B-837	37	1	57	1
	H-005	20	0		
2012	B-830	9	1	43	5
	B-837	25	0		
	H-005	7	4		
	H-007	1	0		
	TW45H	1	0		
2013	B-837	36	4	51	4
	H-005	15	0		
Grand Total 1973–2013				**2808**	**458**

E • Tractors and launch vehicles

Since the Atlantic ILBs have been on station in the early 1970s, a variety of launch vehicles have been used to get the boats afloat. After trials with various second-hand tractors, a Ford County tractor was acquired (right). This was subsequently marinised (below) and numbered TW1 (reg no. XTK 150M), being on station from 1974 to 1987. (By courtesy of New Brighton RNLI)

Above: TW1, after being rebuilt and marinised, recovering Blenwatch (B-549). The modifications allowed the tractor to wade safely to a depth of 1.5m in calm water. (Jeff Morris)

TW17H (reg no. H593 PUX), on station 1990 to 1996, was the first 'bendy' tractor at New Brighton; this type was better suited to the challenging launching conditions on the banks of the Mersey than the less powerful TW1. (Jeff Morris)

Above: TW16H (reg no.H610 SUJ), on station 1996–2001, was the first Talus MB-4H Hydrostatic built by the RNLI and came to New Brighton after three years at Aberdovey in Wales.

TW46H (reg no.V938 EAW), on station 2001–2008, was the station's third Talus MB-4H hydrostatic tractor, and is pictured in 2005 at the end of Coastal Drive; it was sent to Aberystwyth and Rye Harbour after service on Merseyside. The MB-4H is the first tractor to be specifically designed for launching Atlantic ILBs. The vehicle has good ground clearance, steering ability and full waterproofing. After trials around the coast, the first tractor of this type to go on station came to New Brighton in November 1990.

TW45H (reg no.T249 JNT) came on station in 2008; built in 1999, it previously served in Kent at Littlestone-on-Sea.

F • Personnel summary

Honorary Secretaries

H.W. Eddis	1863–1866
Rev R.D. Fowell	1867–1873
John L.C. Hamilton	1873–1890
W.A. Bateson	1890–1891
Hugh B. Kent	1891–1918
Benjamin James Kirkham	1918–1939
W.W. Harris MBE	1939–1954
Capt George Ayre	1954–1962
J. Wallace	1962–1970
W. Duguid	1970–1973
Captain John A. Billington	1973–1990
Peter Shillinglaw	1990–1995
P. Hockey	1995–1996
Frank Brereton	1996–2001
Peter Shillinglaw	2001–2006
A. Calrke (Acting)	2006–2007
C. Downing	2007–2011
G. Sale	2011–

Coxswains

Thomas Evans	1863–1868
Richard J. Thomas	1868–1883
Robert Wilde (note 1)	1883–1887
James Whittle	1887–1892
William Martin	1891–1901
William Cross	3.1901–1920
George Robinson	12.1920–1932
William Henry Jones (note 2)	2.1932–1938
John R. Nicholson MBE	12.1938–1954
George Stonall	1.1955–1962
William Edward Morris	6.1962–1973

Second Coxswains

W. Jones	1875–1883
James Whittle	1883–1894
Samuel Jones	1894–1901
William Bedson	–1920
George Robinson	1911–1920
George Cross	1920–1921
William Henry Jones	1920–1932
John R Nicholson	1921–1938
William Stephen Jones	1938–1962
George Stonall	1945–1955
William Henry Cross	1952–1968
G.H. Cross	1968–1973

Chief Engineers

Arthur Simmons	1893–1917
Alfred Kay	8–9.1917
John Hall	1917–1924

Mechanics

Ralph Brown Scott	1924–1929
Wilfred 'Wally' Garbutt	1929–1944
William MacDonald	1944–1950
Gilbert Barrs	1938–1939
John William Bray	1939–1956
John Charles Bray	1956–1962
Cyril Alcock	1962–1967
Anthony Richardson	1967–1973

Second Mechanics

R. Millmore	1923-1924
Herbert Harrison	1924-25
Wilfred Garbutt	1925-29
J. E. Mason	1929–1940
Claude Norman Wearing	1–2.1940
Edward Downing	1940–1944
Hidden	1944–1945
Laurence Gordon Neil	1945–1949
John Christian	1949–1951
Edwin Williams	1956–1957
F. Neilson	1957–1962
A. Upton	1962–1963
J. Kennedy	1963–1973

Senior Helmsmen

Edward 'Bev' Brown	1973–1986
Clifford Downing	1986–1989
Robert Barrass	1989–1997
Graham Lowe	1997–2004
Michael Jones	2004–2012
David Lowe	2012–

* In retirement while out on his fishing boat with his brother Tom Jones, William Jones fell overboard and drowned. His son, W.S. Jones (Second Coxswain), was in London to receive an award from the RNLI. On his return he searched for the body, which he found by the pier exactly a month later. The committee's retirement present, a silver pocket watch and chain, was with his body, and these were donated to the station in August 2014 as were with his and his son, W.S. Jones', medals and these are now on display in the lifeboat house.

William Cross was Coxswain from March 1901 until 1920. (By courtesy of New Brighton RNLI)

George Robinson, appointed Coxswain in December 1920 and retired in February 1932 through ill health. (By courtesy of the RNLI)

William Henry Jones, Coxswain from February 1932 to 1938. (By courtesy of the RNLI)

John Rowlands Nicholson MBE, Coxswain December 1938 to 1954. (By courtesy of the RNLI)

Coxswain William Jones (centre right, seated wearing cap) and the New Brighton lifeboat crew pictured in the Egerton Street building used as a shore facility in the 1930s. (By courtesy of New Brighton RNLI)

George Stonall, Coxswain January 1955 to June 1962, joined the crew in 1917 and retired 1962, and was a fisherman by trade. (By courtesy of the RNLI)

William Morris took over as Coxswain in June 1962 and was the last person to hold the position. (By courtesy of the RNLI)

Edward 'Bev' Brown, who joined the crew in 1959, was the first senior helmsman on the Atlantic, holding the post from 1973 to 1986. (Courtesy of New Brighton RNLI)

Cliff Downing joined the crew in July 1973, and was senior helmsman from 1986 to 1989. He worked for a local car dealer. (By courtesy of Frank Brereton)

Robert Barrass joined the crew in 1977, became a helm in 1984 and was senior helmsman from 1989 to 1997. (By courtesy of New Brighton RNLI)

Graham Lowe joined the crew in August 1980, was senior helmsman from 1997 to 2004, and became hovercraft commander in 2006. (Nicholas Leach)

Mike Jones joined the crew in 1980, became a helm in 1988 and ILB mechanic in 1997, and was senior helmsman from 2004 to 2012. (Nicholas Leach)

David Lowe joined the crew in 1988, became a helm in 2005 and was appointed senior helmsman in 2012. (Nicholas Leach)